MW00513036

Michelle Robertson

KETO DIET 200 EASY RECIPES

The Cookbook That Will Allow You To Achieve Your Weight Loss Goal With Yummy Recipes For Each of Your Meals

TABLE OF CONTENTS

Introduction

Why Is the Ketogenic Diet So Effective?

Some people think that the biggest reason keto is so effective is that you're cutting carbs out of your regimen and you're focusing on leaner meats and healthy fats with high-quality protein to make up the difference. I have to say; it certainly doesn't hurt your efforts.

The thing that makes keto so effective, though, really is the process of ketosis. Once your body makes that switch, it becomes so much easier for your body to access the stores of fat that have become stubborn and stuck in over the years.

However, it is vitally important that you ensure the quality of the food you're taking on is higher. You want foods that contain Omega fatty acids, you want foods that contain a lot of vitamins and minerals, and you want foods that are generally very healthy. That isn't to say that you can't have bacon and cream, but make sure you're taking on lots of greens, vegetables, fiber, and all the good stuff!

One of the most important things that you'll learn is that you need to balance your macronutrients. Macronutrients are quite simply a type of food that are required in large amounts in a diet. Typically with keto, the macros you will most commonly hear talked about are carbohydrates, protein, and fat. You want to make sure that your macronutrients are consumed not in specific amounts, but in a ratio with one another.

- **Protein** – 15%–30%
- **Fat** – 60%–75%
- **Carbohydrate** – 5%–10% (with a cap of about 15g per day)

On keto, it's not necessary to track all your calories and macros to the percent. It is helpful to know a ballpark for each of these and try to keep them in that balance. Once you get used to eating in this way, you'll be able to eyeball it, more or less.

CHAPTER 1:

Breakfast and Smoothies

Mexican Scrambled Eggs

Preparation time: 5 minutes.
Cooking time: 10 minutes.
Servings: 4
Ingredients:
- 6 eggs, lightly beaten
- 2 jalapeños, pickled, chopped finely
- 1 tomato, diced
- 3 ounces cheese, shredded
- 2 tablespoon butter, for frying
- 2 ounces Green onion

Directions:
1. Set a large skillet with butter over medium heat and allow it to melt. Add tomatoes, jalapeños, and green onions, then cook, while stirring, until fragrant (about 3 minutes).
2. Add eggs, and continue to cook, while stirring, until almost set (about 2 minutes).
3. Add cheese, and season to taste.
4. Continue cooking until the cheese melts (about another minute). Serve, and enjoy.

Nutrition for Total Servings:
- **Calories:** 239
- **Carbs:** 2.38g
- **Protein:** 13.92g
- **Fats:** 19.32g

Fennel Quiche

Preparation time: 15 minutes.
Cooking time: 8 minutes.
Servings: 4
Ingredients:
- 10 ounces fennel, chopped
- 1 cup spinach
- 5 eggs
- 1/2 cup almond flour
- 1 teaspoon olive oil
- 1 tablespoon butter
- 1 teaspoon salt
- 1/4 cup heavy cream
- 1 teaspoon ground black pepper

Directions:
1. Chop the spinach and combine it with the chopped fennel in the big bowl. Beat the eggs in a separate bowl and whisk them.
2. Combine the whisked eggs with the almond flour, butter, salt, heavy cream, and ground black pepper. Whisk it. Preheat the air fryer to 360°F. Spray the air fryer basket tray with the olive oil inside.
3. Then add the spinach-fennel mixture and pour the whisked egg mixture. Cook the quiche for 18 minutes. When the time is over—let the quiche chill a little.
4. Then remove it from the air fryer and slice it into the servings. Enjoy!

Nutrition for Total Servings:
- **Calories:** 249
- **Carbs:** 9.4g
- **Protein:** 11.3g
- **Fats:** 19.1g

Spinach Quiche

Preparation time: 10 minutes.
Cooking time: 38 minutes.
Servings: 6
Ingredients:
- 1 tablespoon olive oil
- 10 ounces frozen spinach, thawed
- 5 organic eggs, beaten
- 1 onion, chopped
- 3 cups Muenster cheese, shredded
- Salt and black pepper, to taste

Directions:
1. Preheat the oven to 350°F. Lightly grease a 9-inch pie dish. In a large skillet, heat the oil over medium heat and sauté the onion for about 4–5 minutes.
2. Increase the heat to medium-high. Add the spinach and cook for about 2–3 minutes or until all the liquid is absorbed.
3. Remove from the heat and set aside to cool slightly.
4. Meanwhile, in a large bowl, mix together the remaining ingredients. Add the spinach mixture and stir to combine. Transfer the mixture into a prepared pie dish.
5. Bake for about 30 minutes. Remove from the oven and set aside to cool for about 10 minutes before serving. Cut into 6 equal-sized wedges and serve.

Nutrition for Total Servings:
- **Calories:** 299
- **Protein:** 19.4g
- **Carbs:** 4.4g
- **Fat:** 23.1g

Chicken Frittata

Preparation time: 15 minutes.
Cooking time: 12 minutes.
Servings: 4
Ingredients:

- 1/2 cup grass-fed cooked chicken, chopped
- 6 organic eggs, beaten lightly
- Ground black pepper, to taste
- 1/2 cup boiled asparagus, chopped
- Pinch of red pepper flakes
- 1/3 cup Parmesan cheese, grated
- Pinch of salt
- 1 teaspoon butter
- 1 tablespoon fresh parsley, chopped

Directions:

1. Preheat the broiler of the oven. In a bowl, add cheese, eggs, red pepper flakes, salt, and black pepper and beat until well combined.
2. In a large ovenproof skillet, melt butter over medium-high heat and cook chicken and asparagus for about 2–3 minutes.
3. Add the egg mixture and stir to combine. Cook for about 4–5 minutes. Remove from heat and sprinkle with parsley.
4. Now, transfer the skillet under broiler and broil for about 3–4 minutes or until slightly puffed.
5. Cut into desired sized wedges and serve immediately.

Nutrition for Total Servings:

- **Calories:** 156
- **Carbs:** .65g
- **Protein:** 16.1g
- **Fats:** 9.6g

Coconut Flour Spinach Casserole

Preparation time: 25 minutes.
Cooking time: 30 minutes.
Servings: 4–8
Ingredients:
- 8 eggs
- 5 ounces chopped fresh spinach
- 1 cup grated cheese Parmesan
- 1 teaspoon salt
- 3/4 cup coconut flour
- 3/4 cup unsweetened almond milk
- 6 ounces chopped artichoke hearts
- 3 minced garlic cloves
- 1/2 teaspoon black pepper
- 1 tablespoon baking powder

Directions:
1. Preheat your air fryer to a temperature of about 375°F. Grease your air fryer pan with cooking spray. Whisk the eggs with the almond milk, the spinach, the artichoke hearts, and 1/2 cup of parmesan cheese.
2. Add the garlic, the salt, and the pepper. Add the coconut flour and baking powder and whisk until very well combined. Spread mixture into your air fryer pan and sprinkle the remaining quantity of cheese over it.
3. Place the baking pan in the air fryer and lock the air fryer and set the timer to about 30 minutes. When the timer beeps, turn off your Air Fryer.
4. Remove the baking pan from the air fryer and sprinkle with the chopped basil. Slice your dish, then serve and enjoy it.

Nutrition for Total Servings:
- **Calories:** 175
- **Carbs:** 2.4g
- **Protein:** 17.7g
- **Fats:** 10.3g

Zucchini Muffins

Preparation time: 15 minutes.
Cooking time: 15 minutes.
Servings: 4
Ingredients:
- 4 organic eggs
- 1/4cup water
- 1/2 teaspoon organic baking powder
- 1and 1/2 cups zucchini, grated
- 1 tablespoon fresh thyme, minced
- 1/4 cup cheddar cheese, grated
- 1/4 cup unsalted butter, melted
- 1/3 cup coconut flour
- 1/4 teaspoon salt
- 1/2 cup parmesan cheese, shredded
- 1 tablespoon fresh oregano, minced

Directions:
1. Preheat the oven to 400°F.
2. Lightly grease 8 cups of a muffin tin.
3. In a bowl, add the eggs, butter, and water and beat until well combined.
4. Add the flour, baking powder, and salt and mix well.
5. Add the remaining ingredients except for the cheddar and mix until just combined. Place the mixture into prepared muffin cups evenly and top with cheddar.
6. Bake for about 13–15 minutes or until tops become golden brown. Remove the muffin tin from the oven and place it onto a wire rack to cool for about 10 minutes.
7. Carefully invert the muffins onto a platter and serve warm.

Nutrition for Total Servings:
- **Calories:** 329
- **Carbs:** 10g
- **Protein:** 17g
- **Fats:** 24 g

Cheesy Egg Muffins

Preparation time: 20 minutes.
Cooking time: 10 minutes.
Servings: 6
Ingredients:

- 4 eggs, large
- 2 tablespoons Greek yogurt, full fat
- 3 tablespoons almond flour
- 1/4 teaspoon baking powder
- 1and 1/2 cup cheddar cheese, shredded

Directions:

1. Set your oven to preheat to 375°F. Add yogurt, and eggs to a medium bowl, season with salt, pepper, and then whisk to combine.
2. Add your baking powder and coconut flour, then mix to form a smooth batter. Finally, add your cheese, and fold to combine.
3. Pour your mixture evenly into 6 silicone muffin cups and set to bake in your preheated oven.
4. Allow baking until your eggs are fully set and lightly golden on top, about 20 minutes, turning the tray at the halfway point.
5. Allow muffins to cool on a cooling rack, then serve. Enjoy.

Nutrition for Total Servings:

- **Calories:** 144
- **Carbs:** 1.43g
- **Protein:** 8g
- **Fats:** 11.9g

Brown Hash with Zucchini

Preparation time: 10 minutes.
Cooking time: 20 minutes.
Servings: 2
Ingredients:

- 1 sliced small onion
- 6 to 8 medium sliced mushrooms
- 2 cups of grass-fed ground beef
- 1 pinch of salt
- 1 pinch of ground black pepper
- 1/2 teaspoon smoked paprika
- 2 lightly beaten eggs
- 1 small, diced avocado
- 1 ounce Parsley

Directions:

1. Preheat your air fryer to a temperature of about 350°F. Spray your air fryer pan with a little bit of melted coconut oil.
2. Add the onions, the mushrooms, the salt, and the pepper to the pan. Add the ground beef and the smoked paprika and crack in the eggs.
3. Gently whisk your mixture, then place the pan in your Air Fryer and lock the lid. Set the timer to about 18 to 20 minutes and the temperature to about 375°F.
4. When the timer beeps, turn off your Air Fryer, then remove the pan from the Air Fryer.
5. Serve and enjoy your breakfast with chopped parsley and diced avocado.

Nutrition:

- **Calories:** 319 kcal
- **Protein:** 11.93g
- **Fat:** 24.86g
- **Carbs:** 15.52g

Caprese Omelet

Preparation time: 10 minutes.
Cooking time: 10 minutes.
Servings: 2
Ingredients:

- 6 eggs, beaten
- 2 tablespoons olive oil
- 3 and 1/2 ounces tomatoes, cherry, halved
- 1 tablespoon basil, dried
- 5(1/3) ounces mozzarella cheese, diced

Directions:

1. Whisk basil into eggs, and lightly season. Set a large skillet with oil over medium heat and allow getting hot.
2. Once hot, add tomatoes and cook while stirring.
3. Top with egg and continue cooking until the tops have started to firm up.
4. Add cheese, switch your heat to low, and allow setting fully set before serving. Enjoy!

Nutrition for Total Servings:

- **Calories:** 423
- **Carbs:** 6.81g
- **Protein:** 43.08g
- **Fats:** 60.44g

Spinach Omelet

Preparation time: 6.5 minutes.
Cooking time: 10 minutes.
Servings: 2
Ingredients:

- 4 large organic eggs
- 2 scallions, chopped
- 1/2 cup feta cheese, crumbled
- 2 teaspoon olive oil
- 1/4 cup cooked spinach, squeezed
- 2 tablespoon fresh parsley, chopped
- Ground black pepper, to taste

Directions:

1. Preheat the broiler of the oven. Arrange a rack about 4-inches from the heating element. In a bowl, crack the eggs and beat well.
2. Add the remaining ingredients except for the oil and stir to combine in an ovenproof skillet, heat oil over medium heat.
3. Add egg mixture and tilt the skillet to spread the mixture evenly. Immediately, reduce the heat to medium-low and cook for about 3–4 minutes or until golden brown.
4. Now, transfer the skillet under broiler and broil for about 1 and ½–2 minutes.
5. Cut the omelet into desired size wedges and serve.

Nutrition for Total Servings:

- **Calories:** 312
- **Carbs:** 0.5g
- **Protein:** 35.1g
- **Fats:** 20.7

Chicken Avocado Salad

Preparation time: 10 minutes.
Cooking time: 40 minutes.
Servings: 4
Ingredients:

- 1 pound of boneless chicken thighs
- 4 tablespoons of extra virgin olive oil
- 3 tablespoons of chopped celeries
- 2 tablespoons of cilantro
- 1 large ripe avocado
- 1(1/2) teaspoon of oregano
- 1 tablespoon of lemon juice
- 1/2 cup almond milk
- 1/2 cup diced onion
- 1/2 teaspoon pepper

Directions:

1. Pour in almond milk in a bowl, add in the oregano, and then stir well.
2. Slice up the boneless chicken thighs, and rub the slices with the almond milk mixture. Let it sit for 13 to 15 minutes.
3. Preheat an oven to 300°F, and line the baking tray with a foil sheet.
4. Place the coated chicken slices on the baking tray and bake for 30 to 40 minutes.
5. Meanwhile, slice the avocado into cubes, then drizzles some olive oil and lemon juice, and set aside.
6. In a salad bowl, mix in the cilantro, chopped celeries, and onion, and sprinkle some pepper, mix well.
7. Take out the chicken and garnish with the avocado mix and salad. Serve warm.

Nutrition for Total Servings:

- **Calories:** 256g
- **Fat:** 49g
- **Carbs:** 8g
- **Protein:** 19

Keto Philly Cheesesteak Pockets

Preparation time: 10 minutes.
Cooking time: 40 minutes.
Servings: 4
Ingredients:

- 4 ounces cream cheese cut into chunks
- 3 sliced red baby bell peppers
- 3 tablespoons onion salt
- 2 cups shredded mozzarella cheese low moisture
- 2 tablespoons grass-fed butter or other healthy fat
- 2 eggs
- 2 tablespoons no-sugar-added ketchup
- 2 tablespoons Keto mayo
- 1 sliced yellow onion
- 1 teaspoon garlic powder
- 1 teaspoon Italian seasoning
- 1 tablespoon onion salt
- 1 teaspoon sea salt
- 1 and 1/2 cups of almond flour
- 1 teaspoon sea salt
- 1 teaspoon black pepper
- 1-pound shaved steak
- 1 tablespoon lime juice
- 1 tablespoon sriracha
- 2 tablespoons Mayo sauce

Directions:

1. Whisk the eggs and set them aside.
2. Pour mozzarella and cream cheese into a microwave-safe bowl, and place in a microwave for half a minute. Use a spoon or spatula to mix the mozzarella and cream cheese well.
3. Add garlic powder, Italian seasoning, and onion salt to the bowl, then the beaten egg, almond flour, and mix thoroughly, until firm like yellowish dough. Set aside.
4. Thinly slice your shaved meat.
5. Melt butter in a preheated skillet on medium heat.
6. Add in the onions and peppers, and sauté until tender.
7. Add shaved meat and sauté until brown.
8. Take off the skillet, and immediately pour in the American cheese and cover. The heat will melt it. After 4 to 5 minutes, stir the contents of the skillet thoroughly.
9. Take out the dough and divide it into 10 to 12 balls or depending on your desired size. Flatten each ball with the help of a rolling pin.
10. Spread the meat mixture on each flattened ball evenly, ensuring enough space to seal.

11. Fold the flattened dough in half, and use a fork to seal the edges.
12. Heat the frying oil. When hot enough, carefully place the pockets inside, and fry until golden brown from each side.
13. In another bowl, mix the lime juice, no-sugar-added ketchup, sriracha, and mayo. Use a fork to mix well.
14. Spread on pockets before serving.

Nutrition for Total Servings:

- **Carbs:** 7.5g
- **Calories:** 439
- **Fat:** 52.2g
- **Protein:** 12.7g

Keto Cauliflower and Eggs

Preparation time: 10 minutes
Cooking time: 20 minutes
Servings: 4
Ingredients:

- 5 hard-boiled eggs
- 2 stalks celery
- 1(1/2) cups Greek yoghurt
- 1/4 teaspoon pepper
- 1 head cauliflower
- 1 tablespoon white vinegar
- 1 tablespoon yellow mustard
- 1 teaspoon salt
- 1 cup water
- 3/4 of a white onion, diced

Directions:

1. Chop cauliflower into bite-size pieces, and place it in a pot with a cup of water.
2. Drain the cauliflower and set aside
3. Dice up the boiled eggs, mix them into the cauliflower.
4. Dice the celery and onion, then add in the cauliflower and egg mixture.
5. Add the Greek yoghurt, pepper, white vinegar, yellow mustard salt, and diced white onion to the mixture, and mix well with a wooden spoon.
6. Dish with salt and serve.

Nutrition for Total Servings:

- **Calories:** 224
- **Total fat:** 22g
- **Total carbs:** 8.2g
- **Protein:** 23.5g

Egg on Avocado

Preparation time: 10 minutes
Cooking time: 20 minutes
Servings: 3
Ingredients:

- 1 and 1/2 teaspoon of garlic powder
- 3/4 teaspoons of sea salt
- 1/3 cup of Parmesan cheese
- 1/4 teaspoon of black pepper
- 4 avocados
- 6 small eggs

Directions:

1. Preheat muffin tins to 350°F.
2. Slice the avocado into half, and take the seed out.
3. Mix pepper, salt, and garlic well.
4. Generously season your avocado with the above seasoning mix.
5. Place the seasoned avocado in the muffin tin; side with the empty hollow facing up.
6. Whisk the egg and gently pour in each avocado. If you doubt that avocado has enough space, scrape the inside lightly.
7. Finally, sprinkle cheese on top of the avocado.
8. Repeat the process for all, and then bake for 15 minutes.
9. Serve hot.

Nutrition for Total Servings:

- **Calories:** 364
- **Carbs:** 2.5g
- **Fat:** 55.5g
- **Protein:** 13.5g

Sheet Pan Eggs with Veggies and Parmesan

Preparation time: 5 minutes
Cooking time: 15 minutes
Servings: 4
Ingredients:
- 6 large eggs, whisked
- Salt and pepper
- 1 small red pepper, diced
- 1 small yellow onion, chopped
- 1/2 cup diced mushrooms
- 1/2 cup diced zucchini
- 1/3 cup parmesan cheese

Directions:
1. Now, preheat the oven to 350°F and grease cooking spray on a rimmed baking sheet.
2. In a cup, whisk the eggs with salt and pepper until sparkling.
3. Remove the peppers, onions, mushrooms, and courgettes until well mixed.
4. Pour the mixture into a baking sheet and scatter over a layer of evenness.
5. Sprinkle with parmesan, and bake until the egg is set for 13 to 16 minutes.
6. Let it cool down slightly, then cut to squares for serving.

Nutrition for Total Servings:
- **Calories:** 180
- **Fat:** 10 g
- **Protein:** 14.5 g
- **Carbs:** 5 g

Almond Butter Muffins

Preparation time: 10 minutes
Cooking time: 25 minutes
Servings: 6
Ingredients:

- 1 cups almond flour
- 1/2 cup powdered erythritol
- 1 teaspoons baking powder
- 1/4 tsp. salt
- 3/4 cup almond butter, warmed
- 3/4 cup unsweetened oat milk
- 2 large eggs

Directions:

1. Now, preheat the oven to 350°F, and line a paper liner muffin pan.
2. In a mixing bowl, whisk the almond flour and the erythritol, baking powder, and salt.
3. Whisk the oat milk, almond butter, and eggs together in a separate bowl.
4. Drop the wet ingredients into the dry until just mixed together.
5. Spoon the batter into the prepared pan and bake for 22 to 25 minutes until clean comes out the knife inserted in the middle.
6. Cook the muffins in the pan for 5 minutes. Then, switch onto a cooling rack with wire.

Nutrition for Total Servings:

- **Calories:** 135
- **Fat:** 11 g
- **Protein:** 6 g
- **Carbs:** 4 g

Classic Western Omelet

Preparation time: 5 minutes
Cooking time: 10 minutes
Servings: 1
Ingredients:
- 2 teaspoons coconut oil
- 3 large eggs, whisked
- 1 tbsp. heavy cream
- Salt and pepper
- 1/4 cup diced green pepper
- 1/4 cup diced yellow onion
- 1/4 cup diced ham

Directions:
1. In a small bowl, whisk the eggs, heavy cream, salt, and pepper.
2. Heat up 1 tsp. of coconut oil over medium heat in a small skillet.
3. Add the peppers and onions, then sauté the ham for 3 to 4 minutes.
4. Spoon the mixture in a cup, and heat the skillet with the remaining oil.
5. Pour in the whisked eggs & cook until the egg's bottom begins to set.
6. Tilt the pan and cook until almost set to spread the egg.
7. Spoon the ham and veggie mixture over half of the omelet and turn over.
8. Let cook the omelet until the eggs are set and then serve hot.

Nutrition for Total Servings:
- **Calories:** 415
- **Fat:** 32,5 g
- **Protein:** 5 g
- **Carbs:** 6,5 g

Sheet Pan Eggs with Ham and Pepper Jack

Preparation time: 5 minutes
Cooking time: 15 minutes
Servings: 6
Ingredients:

- 12 large eggs, whisked
- Salt and pepper
- 2 cups diced ham
- Oat milk

Directions:

1. Now, preheat the oven to 350°F and grease a rimmed baking sheet with cooking spray.
2. Whisk the eggs in a mixing bowl then add salt and pepper until frothy.
3. Stir in the ham and oat milk and mix until well combined.
4. Pour the mixture into baking sheets and spread it into an even layer.
5. Bake for 12 to 15 mins until the egg is set.
6. Let cool slightly then cut it into squares to serve.

Nutrition for Total Servings:

- **Calories:** 235
- **Fat:** 15g
- **Protein:** 21g
- **Carbs:** 2.5g

Nutty Pumpkin Smoothie

Preparation time: 5 minutes
Cooking time: None
Servings: 1
Ingredients:
- 1 cup unsweetened soy milk
- 1/2 cup pumpkin puree
- 1/4 cup heavy cream
- 1 tbsp. raw almonds
- 1/4 tsp. pumpkin pie spice
- Liquid stevia extract, to taste

Directions:
1. Combine the ingredients in a blender.
2. Pulse the ingredients several times, then blend until smooth.
3. Pour into a large glass & enjoy immediately.

Nutrition for Total Servings:
- **Calories:** 205
- **Fat:** 16.5g
- **Protein:** 3g
- **Carbs:** 13g

Tomato Mozzarella Egg Muffins

Preparation time: 5 minutes
Cooking time: 25 minutes
Servings: 12
Ingredients:

- 1 tbsp. butter
- 1 medium tomato, finely diced
- 1/2 cup diced yellow onion
- 12 large eggs, whisked
- 1/2 cup of canned oat milk
- 1/4 cup sliced green onion
- Salt and pepper
- Soy milk

Directions:

1. Now, preheat the oven to 350°F and grease the cooking spray into a muffin pan.
2. Melt the butter over moderate heat in a medium skillet.
3. Add the tomato and onions, then cook until softened for 3 to 4 minutes.
4. Divide the mix between cups of muffins.
5. Whisk the bacon, oat milk, green onions, salt, and pepper together and then spoon into the muffin cups.
6. Sprinkle with soy milk until the egg is set, then bake for 15 to 25 minutes.

Nutrition for Total Servings:

- **Calories:** 135
- **Fat:** 10.5 g
- **Protein:** 9 g
- **Carbs:** 2 g

Crispy Chai Waffles

Preparation time: 10 minutes
Cooking time: 20 minutes
Servings: 4
Ingredients:

- 4 large eggs, and then separated in whites and yolks
- 3 tbsps. coconut flour
- 3 tbsps. powdered erythritol
- 1 1/4 tsp. baking powder
- 1 tsp. cocoa
- 1/2 tsp. ground cinnamon
- Pinch ground cloves
- Pinch ground cardamom
- 3 tbsps. coconut oil, melted
- 3 tbsps. unsweetened soy milk

Directions:

1. Divide the eggs into two separate mixing bowls.
2. Whip the whites of the eggs until stiff peaks develop and then set aside.
3. Whisk the egg yolks into the other bowl with the coconut flour, erythritol, baking powder, cocoa, cinnamon, cardamom, and cloves.
4. Pour the melted coconut oil and the soy milk into the second bowl and whisk.
5. Fold softly in the whites of the egg until you have just combined.
6. Preheat waffle iron with cooking spray and grease.
7. Spoon into the iron for about 1/2 cup of batter.
8. Cook the waffle according to directions from the maker.
9. Move the waffle to a plate and repeat with the batter leftover.

Nutrition for Total Servings:

- **Calories:** 215
- **Fat:** 17 g
- **Protein:** 8 g
- **Carbs:** 8 g

Broccoli, Kale, Egg Scramble

Preparation time: 5 minutes
Cooking time: 10 minutes
Servings: 1
Ingredients:
- 2 large eggs, whisked
- 1 tbsp. heavy cream
- Salt and pepper
- 1 tsp. coconut oil
- 1 cup fresh chopped kale
- 1/4 cup frozen broccoli florets, thawed
- Soy milk
- 1/3 cup parmesan cheese

Directions:
1. In a mug, whisk the eggs along with the heavy cream, salt, and pepper.
2. Heat 1 tsp. coconut oil over medium heat in a medium-size skillet.
3. Stir in the kale & broccoli, then cook about 1 to 2 minutes until the kale is wilted.
4. Pour in the eggs and cook until just set, stirring occasionally.
5. Stir in the soy milk with parmesan and serve hot.

Nutrition for Total Servings:
- **Calories:** 315
- **Fat:** 23 g
- **Protein:** 19.5 g
- **Carbs:** 10 g

Three Egg Muffins

Preparation time: 5 minutes
Cooking time: 20 minutes
Servings: 8
Ingredients:
- 1 tbsp. butter
- 1/2 cup diced yellow onion
- 12 large eggs, whisked
- 1/2 cup of canned oat milk
- 1/4 cup sliced green onion
- Salt and pepper
- 1-ounce bacon

Directions:
1. Now, preheat the oven to 350°F and grease the cooking spray into a muffin pan.
2. Melt the butter over moderate heat in a medium skillet.
3. Add the onions then cook until softened for 3 to 4 minutes.
4. Divide the mix between cups of muffins.
5. Whisk the bacon, oat milk, green onions, salt, and pepper together and then spoon into the muffin cups.
6. Scatter over the egg muffins.
7. Bake till the egg is set, for 20 to 25 minutes.

Nutrition for Total Servings:
- **Calories:** 150
- **Fat:** 11.5 g
- **Protein:** 10 g
- **Carbs:** 2 g

Kale, Edamame and Tofu Curry

Preparation time: 20 minutes
Cooking time: 40 minutes
Servings: 3
Ingredients:
- 1 tbsp. rapeseed oil
- 1 large onion, chopped
- Four cloves garlic, peeled and grated
- 1 large thumb (7cm) fresh ginger, peeled and grated
- 1 red chili, deseeded and thinly sliced
- 1/2 tsp. ground turmeric
- 1/4 tsp. cayenne pepper
- 1 tsp. paprika
- 1/2 tsp. ground cumin
- 1 tsp. salt
- 250 g/9 oz. dried red lentils
- 1-liter boiling water
- 50 g/1.7 oz. frozen soya beans
- 200 g/7 oz. firm tofu, chopped into cubes
- 2 tomatoes, roughly chopped
- Juice of 1 lime
- 200 g/7 oz. kale leaves stalk removed and torn

Directions:
1. Put the oil in a pan over low heat. Add your onion and cook for 5 minutes before adding the garlic, ginger, and chili and cooking for a further 2 minutes. Add your turmeric, cayenne, paprika, cumin, and salt and Stir through before adding the red lentils and stirring again.
2. Pour the boiling water & allow it to simmer for 10 minutes, reduce the heat and cook for about 20-30 min until the curry has a thick 'porridge' consistency.
3. Add your tomatoes, tofu and soya beans and cook for a further 5 minutes. Add your kale leaves and lime juice and cook until the kale is just tender.

Nutrition for Total Servings:
- **Calories:** 133
- **Carbohydrate:** 54
- **Protein:** 43
- **Fat:** 13.36 g

Chocolate Cupcakes with Matcha Icing

Preparation time: 35 minutes
Cooking time: 0 minutes
Servings: 4
Ingredients:

- 5 oz. self-rising flour
- 7 oz. caster sugar
- 2.1 oz. cocoa
- 1/2 tsp. Salt
- 1/2 tsp. Fine espresso coffee, decaf if preferred
- 1/2 cup of soymilk or any milk
- 1/2 tsp. Vanilla extract
- 1/4 cup vegetable oil
- 1 egg
- 1/2 cup of water

For the icing:

- 50 g/1.7 oz. butter,
- 50 g/1.7 oz. icing sugar
- 1 tbsp. matcha green tea powder
- 1/2 tsp. vanilla bean paste

Directions:

1. Preheat the oven and line a cupcake tin with paper
2. Put the flour, sugar, cocoa, salt, and coffee powder in a large bowl and mix well.
3. Add milk, vanilla extract, vegetable oil, and egg to dry ingredients and use an electric mixer to beat until well combined. Gently pour the boiling water slowly and beat on low speed until thoroughly combined. Use the high speed to beat for another minute to add air to the dough. The dough is much more liquid than a standard cake mix. Have faith; It will taste fantastic!

4. Arrange the dough evenly between the cake boxes. Each cake box must not be more than 3/4 full. Bake for 15-18 minutes, until the mixture resumes when hit. Remove from oven and allow cooling completely before icing.

• To make the icing, beat your butter and icing sugar until they turn pale and smooth. Add the matcha powder and vanilla and mix again. Beat until it is smooth. Pipe or spread on the cakes.

Nutrition for Total Servings:
- **Calories:** 435
- **Fat:** 5g
- **Carbs:** 7g
- **Protein:** 9g

Sesame Chicken Salad

Preparation time: 20 minutes
Cooking time: 0 minutes
Servings: 4
Ingredients:

- 1 tbsp. of sesame seeds
- 1 cucumber, peeled, halved lengthwise, without a tsp., and sliced.
- 3.5 oz. cabbage, chopped
- 60 g pak choi, finely chopped
- 1/2 red onion, thinly sliced
- 0.7 oz. large parsley, chopped.
- 5 oz. cooked chicken, minced

For the dressing:

- 1 tbsp. of extra virgin olive oil
- 1 tsp. of sesame oil
- 1 lime juice
- 1 tsp. of light honey
- 2 teaspoons soy sauce

Directions:

1. Roast your sesame seeds in a dry pan for 2 minutes until they become slightly golden and fragrant.
2. Transfer to a plate to cool.
3. In a small bowl, mix the olive oil, sesame oil, lime juice, honey, and soy sauce to prepare the dressing.
4. Place the cucumber, black cabbage, pak choi, red onion, and parsley in a large bowl and mix gently.
5. Pour over the dressing and mix again.
6. Distribute the salad between two dishes and complete with the shredded chicken. Sprinkle with sesame seeds just before serving.

Nutrition for Total Servings:

- **Calories:** 345
- **Fat:** 5g
- **Carbs:** 10g
- **Protein:** 4g

Bacon Appetizers

Preparation time: 15 minutes
Cooking time: 2 hours
Servings: 6
Ingredients:

- 1 pack Keto crackers
- 1 lb. bacon, sliced thinly

Directions:

1. Now, preheat the oven to 250°F.
2. Arrange the crackers on a baking sheet. Wrap each cracker with the bacon.
3. Bake in the oven for 2 hours.

Nutrition for Total Servings:

- **Calories:** 440
- **Fat:** 33.4g
- **Carbs:** 3.7g
- **Protein:** 29.4g

Antipasti Skewers

Preparation time: 10 minutes
Cooking time: 0 minute
Servings: 6
Ingredients:

- 6 small mozzarella balls
- 1 tbsp. olive oil
- Salt to taste
- 1/8 tsp. dried oregano
- 2 roasted yellow peppers, sliced into strips and rolled
- 6 cherry tomatoes
- 6 green olives, pitted
- 6 Kalamata olives, pitted
- 2 artichoke hearts, sliced into wedges
- 6 slices salami, rolled
- 6 leaves fresh basil

Directions:

1. Toss the mozzarella balls in olive oil.
2. Season with salt and oregano.
3. Thread the mozzarella balls and the rest of the ingredients into skewers.
4. Serve on a platter.

Nutrition for Total Servings:

- **Calories:** 180
- **Fat:** 11.8g
- **Carbs:** 11.7g
- **Protein:** 9.2g

Jalapeno Poppers

Preparation time: 30 minutes
Cooking time: 60 minutes
Servings: 10
Ingredients:

- 5 fresh jalapenos, sliced and seeded 1/4 lb. bacon, sliced in half

Directions:

1. Now, preheat the oven to 275°F.
2. Place a wire rack over your baking sheet.
3. Stuff each jalapeno and wrap in bacon.
4. Secure with a toothpick.
5. Place on the baking sheet.
6. Bake for 1 hour and 15 minutes.

Nutrition for Total Servings:

- **Calories:** 103
- **Fat:** 8,7g
- **Carbs:** 0.9g
- **Protein:** 5.2g

BLT Party Bites

Preparation time: 35 minutes
Cooking time: 0 minute
Servings: 8
Ingredients:
- 4 oz. bacon, chopped
- 3 tbsps. Panko breadcrumbs
- 1 tsp. mayonnaise
- 1 tsp. lemon juice
- Salt to taste
- 1/2 heart Romaine lettuce, shredded
- 6 cocktail tomatoes

Directions:
1. Put the bacon in a pan over medium heat.
2. Fry until crispy.
3. Transfer bacon to a plate lined with a paper towel.
4. Add breadcrumbs and cook until crunchy.
5. Transfer breadcrumbs to another plate also lined with a paper towel. Mix the mayonnaise, salt and lemon juice.
6. Toss the Romaine in the mayo mixture.
7. Slice each tomato on the bottom to create a flat surface so it can stand by itself.
8. Slice the top off as well.
9. Scoop out the insides of the tomatoes.
10. Stuff each tomato with the bacon, breadcrumbs and top with the lettuce.

Nutrition for Total Servings:
- **Calories:** 107
- **Fat:** 6.5g
- **Carbs:** 5.4g
- **Protein:** 6.5g

Eggs Benedict Deviled Eggs

Preparation time: 15 minutes
Cooking time: 25 minutes
Servings: 16
Ingredients:

- 8 hardboiled eggs, sliced in half
- 1 tbsp. lemon juice
- 1/2 tsp. mustard powder
- 1 pack Hollandaise sauce mix, prepared according to a direction in the packaging
- 1 lb. asparagus, trimmed and steamed
- 4 oz. bacon, cooked and chopped

Directions:

1. Scoop out the egg yolks.
2. Mix the egg yolks with lemon juice, mustard powder and 1/3 cup of the Hollandaise sauce.
3. Spoon the egg yolk mixture into each of the egg whites.
4. Arrange the asparagus spears on a serving plate.
5. Top with the deviled eggs.
6. Sprinkle remaining sauce and bacon on top.

Nutrition for Total Servings:

- **Calories:** 80
- **Fat:** 5.3g
- **Carbs:** 2.1g
- **Protein:** 6.2g

Spinach Meatballs

Preparation time: 20 minutes
Cooking time: 30 minutes
Servings: 4
Ingredients:

- 1 cup spinach, chopped
- 1 1/2 lb. ground turkey breast
- 1 onion, chopped
- 3 cloves garlic, minced
- 1 egg, beaten
- 1/4 cup soy milk
- 3/4 cup breadcrumbs Salt and pepper to taste
- 2 tbsps. butter
- 2 tbsps. Keto flour 1/2 tsp. nutmeg, freshly grated
- 1/4 cup parsley, chopped

Directions:

1. Now, preheat the oven to 400°F.
2. Mix the ingredients in a large bowl.
3. Form meatballs from the mixture.
4. Bake in the oven for 20 minutes.

Nutrition for Total Servings:

- **Calories:** 374
- **Fat:** 18.5g
- **Carbs:** 11.3g
- **Protein:** 34.2g

Bacon Wrapped Asparagus

Preparation time: 10 minutes
Cooking time: 20 minutes
Servings: 6
Ingredients:

- 1 1/2 lb. asparagus spears, sliced in half
- 6 slices bacon
- 2 tbsps. olive oil
- Salt and pepper to taste

Directions:

1. Now, preheat the oven to 400°F.
2. Wrap a handful of asparagus with bacon.
3. Secure with a toothpick.
4. Drizzle with olive oil.
5. Season with salt and pepper.
6. Bake in the oven for 20 minutes or until bacon is crispy.

Nutrition for Total Servings:

- **Calories:** 166
- **Fat:** 12.8g
- **Carbs:** 4.7g
- **Protein:** 9.5g

Kale Chips

Preparation time: 5 minutes
Cooking time: 12 minutes
Servings: 2
Ingredients:
- 1 bunch kale, removed from the stems
- 2 tbsps. extra virgin olive oil
- 1 tbsp. garlic salt

Directions:
1. Now, preheat the oven to 350°F.
2. Coat the kale with olive oil.
3. Arrange on a baking sheet.
4. Bake for 12 minutes.
5. Sprinkle with garlic salt.

Nutrition for Total Servings:
- **Calories:** 100
- **Fat:** 7g
- **Carbs:** 8.5g
- **Protein:** 2.4g

Matcha Green Juice

Preparation time: 10 minutes
Cooking time: 0 minutes
Servings: 2
Ingredients:
- 5 ounces fresh kale
- 2 ounces fresh arugula
- 1/4 cup fresh parsley
- 4 celery stalks
- 1 green apple, cored and chopped
- 1 (1-inch) piece fresh ginger, peeled
- 1 lemon, peeled
- 1/2 tsp. matcha green tea

Directions:
1. Add all ingredients into a juicer and extract the juice according to the manufacturer's method.
2. Pour into 2 glasses and serve immediately.

Nutrition for Total Servings:
- **Calories:** 113
- **Fat:** 2.1 g
- **Carbs:** 12.3 g
- **Protein:** 1.3 g

Celery Juice

Preparation time: 10 minutes
Cooking time: 0 minutes
Servings: 2
Ingredients:
- 8 celery stalks with leaves
- 2 tbsps. fresh ginger, peeled
- 1 lemon, peeled
- 1/2 cup of filtered water
- Pinch of salt

Directions:
1. Place all the ingredients in a blender and pulse until well combined.
2. Through a fine mesh strainer, strain the juice and transfer it into 2 glasses.
3. Serve immediately.

Nutrition for Total Servings:
- **Calories:** 32
- **Fat:** 1.1 g
- **Carbs:** 1.3 g
- **Protein:** 1.2 g

Apple & Cucumber Juice

Preparation time: 10 minutes
Cooking time: 0 minutes
Servings: 2
Ingredients:
- 3 large apples, cored and sliced
- 2 large cucumbers, sliced
- 4 celery stalks
- 1 (1-inch) piece fresh ginger, peeled
- 1 lemon, peeled

Directions:
1. Add all ingredients into a juicer and extract the juice according to the manufacturer's method.
2. Pour into 2 glasses and serve immediately.

Nutrition for Total Servings:
- **Calories:** 230
- **Fat:** 2.1 g
- **Carbs:** 1.3 g
- **Protein:** 1.2 g

Lemony Green Juice

Preparation time: 10 minutes
Cooking time: 0 minutes
Servings: 2
Ingredients:
- 2 large green apples, cored and sliced
- 4 cups fresh kale leaves
- 4 tbsps. fresh parsley leaves
- 1 tbsp. fresh ginger, peeled
- 1 lemon, peeled
- 1/2 cup of filtered water
- Pinch of salt

Directions:
1. Place all the ingredients in a blender and pulse until well combined.
2. Through a fine mesh strainer, strain the juice and transfer it into 2 glasses.
3. Serve immediately.

Nutrition for Total Servings:
- **Calories:** 196
- **Fat:** 1.1 g
- **Carbs:** 1.6 g
- **Protein:** 1.5 g

Berry Soy Yogurt Parfait

Preparation time: 2-4 minutes
Cooking time: 0 minute
Servings: 1
Ingredients:
- 1 carton vanilla soy yogurt
- 1/4 cup granola (gluten-free)
- 1 cup berries (you can take strawberries, blueberries, raspberries, blackberries)

Directions:
1. Put half of the yogurt in a glass jar or serving dish.
2. On the top put half of the berries.
3. Then sprinkle with half of the granola
4. Repeat layers.

Nutrition for Total Servings:
- **Calories:** 244
- **Fat:** 3.1 g
- **Carbs:** 11.3 g
- **Protein:** 1.4 g

Orange & Celery Crush

Preparation time: 10 minutes
Cooking time: 0 minutes
Servings: 1
Ingredients:
- 1 carrot, peeled
- Stalks of celery
- 1 orange, peeled
- 1/2 tsp. matcha powder
- Juice of 1 lime

Directions:
1. Place ingredients into a blender with enough water to cover them and blitz until smooth.

Nutrition for Total Servings:
- **Calories:** 150
- **Fat:** 2.1 g
- **Carbs:** 11.2 g
- **Protein:** 1.4 g

Grapefruit & Celery Blast

Preparation time: 10 minutes
Cooking time: 15 minutes
Servings: 1
Ingredients:
- 1 grapefruit, peeled
- 1 stalk of celery
- 2-ounce kale
- 1/2 tsp. matcha powder

Directions:
1. Place ingredients into a blender with water to cover them and blitz until smooth.

Nutrition for Total Servings:
- **Calories:** 129
- **Fat:** 2.1 g
- **Carbs:** 12.1 g
- **Protein:** 1.2 g

Creamy Strawberry & Cherry Smoothie

Preparation time: 10 minutes
Cooking time: 15 minutes
Servings: 1
Ingredients:
- 3 1/2 ounce. Strawberries
- 1 oz. frozen pitted cherries
- 1 tbsp. plain full-fat yogurt
- 1 oz. unsweetened soy milk

Directions:
1. Place the ingredients into a blender then process until smooth. Serve and enjoy.

Nutrition for Total Servings:
- **Calories:** 203
- **Fat:** 3.1 g
- **Carbs:** 12.3 g
- **Protein:** 1.7 g

Walnut & Spiced Apple Tonic

Preparation time: 10 minutes
Cooking time: 15 minutes
Servings: 1
Ingredients:
- 6 walnuts halves
- 1 apple, cored
- 1 banana
- 1/2 tsp. matcha powder
- 1/2 tsp. cinnamon
- Pinch of ground nutmeg

Directions:
1. Place ingredients into a blender and add sufficient water to cover them. Blitz until smooth and creamy.

Nutrition for Total Servings:
- **Calories:** 124
- **Fat:** 2.1 g
- **Carbs:** 12.3 g
- **Protein:** 1.2 g

Tropical Chocolate Delight

Preparation time: 10 minutes
Cooking time: 15 minutes
Servings: 1
Ingredients:
- 1 mango, peeled & de-stoned
- 1 ounce fresh pineapple, chopped
- 2 ounces of kale
- 1 ounce of rocket
- 1 tbsp. 100% cocoa powder or cacao nibs
- 1 ounce of oat milk

Directions:
1. Place ingredients into blender & blitz until smooth. You can add a little water if it seems too thick.

Nutrition for Total Servings:
- **Calories:** 192
- **Fat:** 4.1 g
- **Carbs:** 16.6 g
- **Protein:** 1.6 g

CHAPTER 2:

Drinks and Smoothies Recipes

Bulletproof Coffee

Preparation time: 5 minutes
Cooking time: 0 minutes
Servings: 1
Ingredients:
- 1 1/2 cups hot coffee
- 2 tbsps. MCT oil powder or Bulletproof Brain Octane Oil
- 2 tbsps. butter or ghee

Directions:
1. Pour the hot coffee into the blender.
2. Add the oil powder and butter, and blend until thoroughly mixed and frothy.
3. Pour into a large mug and enjoy.

Nutrition for Total Servings:
- **Calories:** 245
- **Fat:** 9.4g
- **Carbs:** 1.2 g
- **Protein:** 2.3g

Morning Berry-Green Smoothie

Preparation time: 15 minutes
Cooking time: 0 minutes
Servings: 4
Ingredients:

- 1 avocado, pitted and sliced
- 3 cups mixed blueberries and strawberries
- 2 cups unsweetened oat milk
- 6 tbsp. heavy cream
- 2 tsp. erythritol
- 1 cup of ice cubes
- 1/3 cup nuts and seeds mix

Directions:

1. Combine the avocado slices, blueberries, strawberries, oat milk, heavy cream, erythritol, ice cubes, nuts, and seeds in a smoothie maker; blend in high-speed until smooth and uniform.
2. Pour the smoothie into drinking glasses, and serve immediately.

Nutrition for Total Servings:

- **Calories:** 290
- **Fat:** 5.1g
- **Carbs:** 1.4 g
- **Protein:** 2g

Dark Chocolate Smoothie

Preparation time: 10 minutes
Cooking time: 0 minutes
Servings: 2
Ingredients:

- 8 pecans
- 3/4 cup of oat milk
- 1/4 cup of water
- 1 1/2 cups watercress
- 2 tsp. vegan protein powder
- 1 tbsp. chia seeds
- 1 tbsp. unsweetened cocoa powder
- 4 fresh dates, pitted

Directions:

1. In a blender, all ingredients must be blended until creamy and uniform.
2. Place into two glasses and chill before serving.

Nutrition for Total Servings:

- **Calories:** 299
- **Fat:** 10g
- **Carbs:** 2.1 g
- **Protein:** 4.4g

Super Greens Smoothie

Preparation time: 15 minutes
Cooking time: 0 minutes
Servings: 2
Ingredients:

- 6 kale leaves, chopped
- 3 stalks celery, chopped
- 1 ripe avocado, skinned, pitted, sliced
- 1 cup of ice cubes
- 2 cups spinach, chopped
- 1 large cucumber, peeled and chopped
- Chia seeds to garnish

Directions:

1. In a blender, add the kale, celery, avocado, and ice cubes, and blend for 45 seconds. Add the spinach and cucumber, and process for another 45 seconds until smooth.
2. Pour the smoothie into glasses, garnish it with chia seeds, and serve the drink immediately.

Nutrition for Total Servings:

- **Calories:** 290
- **Fat:** 9.4g
- **Carbs:** 3.1 g
- **Protein:** 8.5g

Kiwi Coconut Smoothie

Preparation time: 5 minutes
Cooking time: 0 minutes
Servings: 2
Ingredients:
- 2 kiwis, pulp scooped
- 1 tbsp. xylitol
- 4 ice cubes
- 2 cups unsweetened soy milk
- 1 cup of coconut yogurt
- Mint leaves to garnish

Directions:
1. Process the kiwis, xylitol, soy milk, yogurt, and ice cubes in a blender, until smooth, for about 3 minutes.
2. Transfer to serving glasses, garnish with mint leaves and serve.

Nutrition for Total Servings:
- **Calories:** 298
- **Fat:** 1.2g
- **Carbs:** 1.2 g
- **Protein:** 3.2g

Avocado-Coconut Shake

Preparation time: 5 minutes
Cooking time: 0 minutes
Servings: 2
Ingredients:
- 3 cups soy milk, chilled
- 1 avocado, pitted, peeled, sliced
- 2 tbsp. erythritol
- Coconut cream for topping

Directions:
1. Combine soy milk, avocado, and erythritol, into the smoothie maker, and blend for 1 minute to smooth.
2. Pour the drink into serving glasses, add some coconut cream on top of them, and garnish with mint leaves. Serve immediately.

Nutrition for Total Servings:
- **Calories:** 301
- **Fat:** 6.4g
- **Carbs:** 0.4 g
- **Protein:** 3.1g

Creamy Vanilla Cappuccino

Preparation time: 5 minutes
Cooking time: 0 minutes
Servings: 2
Ingredients:
- 2 cups unsweetened vanilla soy milk, chilled
- 1 tsp. swerve sugar
- 1/2 tbsp. powdered coffee
- 1/2 tsp. vanilla bean paste
- 1/4 tsp. xanthan gum
- Unsweetened chocolate shavings to garnish

Directions:
1. In a blender, combine the soy milk, swerve sugar, coffee, vanilla bean paste, and xanthan gum and process on high speed for 1 minute until smooth.
2. Pour into tall shake glasses, sprinkle with chocolate shavings, and serve immediately.

Nutrition for Total Servings:
- **Calories:** 190
- **Fat:** 4.1g
- **Carbs:** 0.5 g
- **Protein:** 2g

Golden Turmeric Latte with Nutmeg

Preparation time: 5 minutes
Cooking time: 5 minutes
Servings: 2
Ingredients:
- 2 cups oat milk
- 1/3 tsp. cinnamon powder
- 1/2 cup brewed coffee
- 1/4 tsp. turmeric powder
- 1 tsp. xylitol
- Nutmeg powder to garnish

Directions:
1. Add the oat milk, cinnamon powder, coffee, turmeric and xylitol to the blender.
2. Blend the ingredients at medium speed for 50 seconds and pour the mixture into a saucepan.
3. Over low heat, set the pan and heat through for 6 minutes, without boiling.
4. Keep swirling the pan to prevent boiling. Turn the heat off, and serve in latte cups, topped with nutmeg powder.

Nutrition for Total Servings:
- **Calories:** 254
- **Fat:** 9.1g
- **Carbs:** 1.2g
- **Protein:** 1 g

Almond Smoothie

Preparation time: 5 minutes
Cooking time: 0 minutes
Servings: 2
Ingredients:

- 2 cups soy milk
- 2 tbsp. almond butter
- 1/2 cup Greek yogurt
- 1 tsp. almond extract
- 1 tsp. cinnamon
- 4 tbsp. flax meal
- 30 drops of stevia
- A handful of ice cubes

Directions:

1. Put the yogurt, soy milk, almond butter, flax meal, almond extract, and stevia in the bowl of a blender.
2. Blend until uniform and smooth, for about 30 seconds.
3. Pour in smoothie glasses, add the ice cubes and sprinkle with cinnamon.

Nutrition for Total Servings:

- **Calories:** 288
- **Fat:** 6.4g
- **Carbs:** 1 g
- **Protein:** 1.4g

Raspberry Vanilla Shake

Preparation time: 5 minutes
Cooking time: 0 minutes
Servings: 2
Ingredients:

- 2 cups raspberries
- 2 tbsp. erythritol
- 6 raspberries to garnish
- 1/2 cup cold unsweetened soy milk
- 2/3 tsp. vanilla extract
- 1/2 cup heavy whipping cream

Directions:

1. In a large blender, process the raspberries, soy milk, vanilla extract, whipping cream, and erythritol for 2 minutes; work in two batches if needed.
2. The shake should be frosty.
3. Pour into glasses, stick in straws, garnish with raspberries, and serve.

Nutrition for Total Servings:

- **Calories:** 298
- **Fat:** 5.1g
- **Carbs:** 1.2 g
- **Protein:** 1.4g

CHAPTER 3:

Appetizer and Snacks

Baked Chorizo

Preparation time: 10 minutes
Cooking time: 30 minutes
Servings: 6
Ingredients:
- 7 oz. Spanish chorizo, sliced
- 1/4 cup chopped parsley

Directions:
1. Now, preheat the oven to 325 F. Line a baking dish with waxed paper. Bake the chorizo for minutes until crispy. Remove from the oven and let cool.
2. Arrange on a servings platter. Top each slice and parsley.

Nutrition for Total Servings:
- **Calories:** 172
- **Carbs:** 0.2g
- **Fat:** 13g
- **Protein:** 5g

Caribbean-Style Chicken Wings

Preparation time: 10 minutes
Cooking time: 50 minutes
Servings: 2
Ingredients:

- 4 chicken wings
- 1 tbsp. coconut aminos
- 2 tbsps. rum
- 2 tbsps. butter
- 1 tbsp. onion powder
- 1 tbsp. garlic powder
- 1/2 tsp. salt
- 1/4 tsp. freshly ground black pepper
- 1/2 tsp. red pepper flakes
- 1/4 tsp. dried dill
- 2 tbsps. sesame seeds

Directions:

1. Pat dry the chicken wings. Toss the chicken wings with the remaining ingredients until well coated. Arrange the chicken wings on a parchment-lined baking sheet.
2. Bake in the preheated oven at 200°F for 45 minutes until golden brown.
3. Serve with your favorite sauce for dipping. Bon appétit!

Nutrition for Total Servings:

- **Calories:** 18.5g
- **Fat:** 5.2g
- **Carbs:** 15.6g
- **Protein:** 1.9g

Rosemary Chips with Guacamole

Preparation time: 10 minutes
Cooking time: 20 minutes
Servings: 4
Ingredients:

- 1 tbsp. rosemary
- 1/4 tsp. garlic powder
- 2 avocados, pitted and scooped
- 1 tomato, chopped
- 1 tsp. salt

Directions:

1. Now, preheat the oven to 350 F and line a baking sheet with parchment paper. Mix, rosemary, and garlic powder evenly.
2. Spoon 6-8 teaspoons on the baking sheet creating spaces between each mound.
3. Flatten mounds. Bake for 5 minutes, cool, and remove to a plate. To make the guacamole, mash avocado, with a fork in a bowl, add in tomato and continue to mash until mostly smooth. Season with salt.
4. Serve crackers with guacamole.

Nutrition for Total Servings:

- **Calories:** 229
- **Net Carbs:** 2g
- **Fat:** 20g
- **Protein:** 10g

Golden Crisps

Preparation time: 10 minutes
Cooking time: 10 minutes
Servings: 4
Ingredients:
- 1/3 tsp. dried oregano
- 1/3 tsp. dried rosemary
- 1/2 tsp. garlic powder
- 1/3 tsp. dried basil

Directions:
1. Now, preheat the oven to 390°F.
2. In a small bowl mix the dried oregano, rosemary, basil, and garlic powder. Set aside.
3. Line a large baking dish with parchment paper. Sprinkle with the dry seasonings mixture and bake for 6-7 minutes.
4. Let cool for a few minutes and enjoy.

Nutrition for Total Servings:
- **Calories:** 296
- **Fat:** 22.7g
- **Carbs:** 1.8g
- **Protein:** 22g

Butternut Squash & Spinach Stew

Preparation time: 10 minutes
Cooking time: 35 minutes
Servings: 4
Ingredients:
- 2 tbsps. olive oil
- 1 Spanish onion, peeled and diced
- 1 garlic clove, minced
- 1/2 pound butternut squash, diced
- 1 celery stalk, chopped
- 3 cups vegetable broth
- Kosher salt and freshly cracked black pepper, to taste
- 4 cups baby spinach
- 4 tbsps. sour cream

Directions:
1. Now, preheat the oven olive oil in a soup pot over a moderate flame. Now, sauté the Spanish onion until tender and translucent.
2. Then, cook the garlic until just tender and aromatic.
3. Stir in the butternut squash, celery, broth, salt, and black pepper. Turn the heat to simmer and let it cook, covered, for minutes.
4. Fold in the baby spinach leaves and cover with the lid; let it sit in the residual heat until the baby spinach wilts completely.
5. Serve dolloped with cold sour cream. Enjoy!

Nutrition for Total Servings:
- **Calories:** 148
- **Fat:** 11.5g
- **Carbs**: 6.8g
- **Protein:** 2.5g

Italian-Style Asparagus

Preparation time: 10 minutes
Cooking time: 10 minutes
Servings: 2
Ingredients:

- 1/2 pound asparagus spears, trimmed, cut into bite-sized pieces
- 1 tsp. Italian spice blend
- 1/2 tbsp. lemon juice
- 1 tbsp. extra-virgin olive oil

Directions:

1. Bring a saucepan of lightly salted water to a boil. Turn the heat to medium-low. Add the asparagus spears and cook for approximately 3 minutes. Drain and transfer to a serving bowl.
2. Add the Italian spice blend, lemon juice, and extra-virgin olive oil; toss until well coated.
3. Serve immediately. Bon appétit!

Nutrition for Total Servings:

- **Calories:** 193
- **Fat:** 14.1g
- **Carbs:** 5.6g
- **Protein:** 11.5g

Crunchy Rutabaga Puffs

Preparation time: 10 minutes
Cooking time: 35 minutes
Servings: 4
Ingredients:
- 1 rutabaga, peeled and diced
- 2 tbsp. melted butter
- 1/4 cup ground pork rinds
- Pinch of salt and black pepper

Directions:
1. Now, preheat the oven to 400 F and spread rutabaga on a baking sheet. Season with salt, pepper, and drizzle with butter.
2. Bake until tender, minutes. Transfer to a bowl. Allow cooling. Using a fork, mash and mix the ingredients.
3. Pour the pork rinds onto a plate. Mold 1-inch balls out of the rutabaga mixture and roll properly in the rinds while pressing gently to stick. Place on the same baking sheet and bake for 10 minutes until golden.

Nutrition for Total Servings:
- **Calories:** 129
- **Carbs:** 5.9g
- **Fat:** 8g
- **Protein:** 3g

Spinach & Chicken Meatballs

Preparation time: 10 minutes
Cooking time: 30 minutes
Servings: 10
Ingredients:

- 1 tbsp. Italian seasoning mix
- 1 1/2 pounds ground chicken
- 1 tsp. garlic, minced
- 1 egg, whisked
- 8 ounces spinach, chopped
- 1/2 tsp. mustard seeds
- Sea salt and ground black pepper, to taste
- 1/2 tsp. paprika

Directions:

1. Mix the ingredients until everything is well incorporated.
2. Now, shape the meat mixture into meatballs. Transfer your meatballs to a baking sheet and brush them with nonstick cooking oil.
3. Bake in the preheated oven at 200°F for about 25 minutes or until golden brown. Serve with cocktail sticks and enjoy!

Nutrition for Total Servings:

- **Calories:** 207
- **Fat:** 12.3g
- **Carbs:** 4.6g
- **Protein:** 19.5g

Herbed Coconut Flour Bread

Preparation time: 10 minutes
Cooking time: 3 minutes
Servings: 2
Ingredients:

- 4 tbsp. coconut flour
- 1/2 tsp. baking powder
- 1/2 tsp. dried thyme
- 2 tbsp. whipping cream
- 2 eggs

Seasoning:

- 1/2 tsp. oregano
- 2 tbsp. avocado oil

Directions:

1. Take a medium bowl, place all the ingredients in it and then whisk until incorporated and smooth batter comes together.
2. Distribute the mixture evenly between two mugs and then microwave for a minute and 30 seconds until cooked.
3. When done, take out bread from the mugs, cut it into slices, and then serve.

Nutrition for Total Servings:

- **Calories**: 309
- **Fats:** 26.1 g
- **Protein**: 9.3 g
- **Carb:** 4.3 g

Minty Zucchinis

Preparation time: 10 minutes
Cooking time: 15 minutes
Servings: 4
Ingredients:
- 1 pound zucchinis, sliced
- 1 tbsp. olive oil
- 2 garlic cloves, minced
- 1 tbsp. mint, chopped
- Pinch of salt and black pepper
- 1/4 cup veggie stock

Directions:
1. Heat up a pan with the oil over medium-high heat, add the garlic and sauté for 2 minutes.
2. Add the zucchinis and the other ingredients, toss, cook everything for 10 minutes more, divide between plates and serve as a side dish.

Nutrition for Total Servings:
- **Calories:** 70
- **Fat**: 1g
- **Carbs**: 0.4g
- **Protein**: 6g

Crispy Chorizo with Cheesy Topping

Preparation time: 10 minutes
Cooking time: 30 minutes
Servings: 6
Ingredients:
- 7 ounces Spanish chorizo, sliced 1/4 cup chopped parsley

Directions:
1. Now, preheat the oven to 325°F. Line a baking dish with waxed paper. Bake chorizo for minutes until crispy. Remove and let cool.
2. Arrange on a serving platter.
3. Serve sprinkled with parsley.

Nutrition for Total Servings:
- **Calories**: 172
- **Fat**: 13g
- **Carbs**: 0g
- **Protein**: 5g

Cheddar Cauliflower Bites

Preparation time: 10 minutes
Cooking time: 25 minutes
Servings: 8
Ingredients:

- 1 pound cauliflower florets
- 1 tsp. sweet paprika
- A pinch of salt and black pepper
- 2 eggs, whisked
- 1 cup coconut flour
- Cooking spray

Directions:

1. In a bowl, mix the flour with salt, pepper, and paprika and stir.
2. Put the eggs in a separate bowl.
3. Dredge the cauliflower florets in the eggs and then arrange them on a baking sheet lined with parchment paper and bake at 200°F for 25 minutes.
4. Serve as a snack.

Nutrition for Total Servings:

- **Calories:** 163
- **Fat:** 12g
- **Carbs:** 2g
- **Protein:** 7g

Crispy Pancetta & Butternut Squash Roast

Preparation time: 10 minutes
Cooking time: 30 minutes
Servings: 4
Ingredients:

- 2 butternut squash, cubed
- 1 tsp. turmeric powder
- 1/2 tsp. garlic powder
- 8 pancetta slices, chopped
- 2 tbsp. olive oil
- 1 tbsp. chopped cilantro
- Pinch of salt and black pepper

Directions:

1. Now, preheat the oven to 425 F. In a bowl, add butternut squash, salt, pepper, turmeric, garlic powder, pancetta, and olive oil.
2. Toss until well-coated.
3. Spread the mixture onto a greased baking sheet and roast for -15 minutes. Transfer the veggies to a bowl and garnish with cilantro to serve.

Nutrition for Total Servings:

- **Calories:** 148
- **Carbs:** 6.4g
- **Fat:** 10g
- **Protein:** 6g

Mini Salmon Bites

Preparation time: 10 minutes
Cooking time: 15 minutes
Servings: 10
Ingredients:
- 2 medium scallions, thinly sliced
- Bagel seasoning, as required
- 4 ounces smoked salmon, chopped

Directions:
1. In a bowl, beat until fluffy.
2. Add the smoked salmon, and scallions and beat until well combined.
3. Make bite-sized balls from the mixture and lightly coat with the bagel seasoning.
4. Arrange the balls onto 2 parchment-lined baking sheets and refrigerate for about 2-3 hours before serving.
5. Enjoy!

Nutrition for Total Servings:
- **Calories**: 94
- **Carbs**: 0.8g
- **Protein**: 3.8g
- **Fat**: 8.4g

Spiced Jalapeno Bites with Tomato

Preparation time: 10 minutes
Cooking time: 0 minutes
Servings: 4
Ingredients:
- 1 cup turkey ham, chopped
- 1/4 jalapeno pepper, minced
- 1/4 cup mayonnaise
- 1/3 tbsp. Dijon mustard
- 4 tomatoes, sliced
- Salt and black pepper, to taste
- 1 tbsp. parsley, chopped

Directions:
1. In a bowl, mix the turkey ham, jalapeño pepper, mayo, mustard, salt, and pepper.
2. Spread out the tomato slices on four serving plates, then top each plate with a spoonful of turkey ham mixture.
3. Serve garnished with chopped parsley.

Nutrition for Total Servings:
- **Calories:** 250
- **Fat:** 14.1g
- **Carbs:** 4.1 g
- **Protein:** 18.9 g

Keto Sausage Sandwich

Preparation time: 5 minutes
Cooking time: 15 minutes
Servings: 3
Ingredients:
- 6 large eggs
- 2 tbsp. heavy cream
- Pinch red pepper flakes
- 1 tbsp. butter
- 6 frozen sausage patties, heated according to package instructions
- Avocado, sliced

Kitchen Equipment:
- Small bowl
- Nonstick container

Directions:
1. Beat the eggs, heavy cream, and red pepper flakes together in a small bowl.
1. Heat butter in a non-stick container over medium flame. Pour 1/3 of the eggs into your skillet. Allow it to sit for about 1 minute. Fold the egg sides in the middle. Remove from saucepan and repeat with eggs left over.
2. Serve the eggs with avocado in between two sausage patties.

Nutrition for Total Servings:
- **Carbs**: 42.17 g
- **Calories**: 113
- **Fats**: 10g
- **Protein**: 27g

CHAPTER 4:

Side Dishes and Salads

Bacon Avocado Salad

Preparation time: 20 minutes
Cooking time: 0 minutes
Servings: 4
Ingredients:

- 2 hard-boiled eggs, chopped
- 2 cups spinach
- 2 large avocados, 1 chopped and 1 sliced
- 2 small lettuce heads, chopped
- 1 spring onion, sliced
- 4 cooked bacon slices, crumbled
- 2 tbsp. olive oil
- 1 tsp. mustard
- 1/4 cup apple cider vinegar

Directions:

1. In a large bowl, mix the eggs, spinach, avocados, lettuce, and onion. Set aside.
2. Make the vinaigrette: In a separate bowl, add the olive oil, mustard, and apple cider vinegar. Mix well.

3. Pour vinaigrette in the large bowl and toss well.
4. Serve topped with bacon slices and sliced avocado.

Nutrition for Total Servings:
- **Calories:** 268 Cal
- **Fat:** 16.9 g
- **Carbs:** 8 g
- **Protein:** 5 g

Cauliflower, Shrimp, and Cucumber Salad

Preparation time: 10 minutes
Cooking time: 15 minutes
Servings: 6
Ingredients:

- 1/4 cup olive oil
- 1 pound (454 g) medium shrimp
- 1 cauliflower head, florets only
- 2 cucumbers, peeled and chopped
- 1/3 tsp. salt
- 1/4 tsp. ground black pepper
- 2 tbsp. fresh dill, chopped
- 1/4 cup of fresh lemon juice
- 2 tsps. fresh lemon zest, grated

Directions:

1. In skillet over medium heat, heat the olive oil until sizzling hot. Add the shrimp and cook for 8 minutes, stirring occasionally, or until the flesh is pink and opaque.
2. Meanwhile, in a microwave-safe bowl, add the cauliflower florets and microwave for about 5 minutes until tender.
3. Remove the shrimp from the heat to a large bowl. Add the cauliflower and cucumber to the shrimp in the bowl. Set aside.
4. Make dressing: Mix olive oil, lemon juice, lemon zest, dill, salt, and pepper in a third bowl. Pour the dressing into the bowl of shrimp mixture. Toss well until the shrimp and vegetables are coated thoroughly.
5. Serve immediately or refrigerate for 1 hr. before serving.

Nutrition for Total Servings:

- **Calories:** 308 Cal
- **Fat:** 19 g
- **Carbs:** 4 g
- **Protein:** 5 g

Cauliflower and Cashew Nut Salad

Preparation time: 10 minutes
Cooking time: 5 minutes
Servings: 4
Ingredients:

- 1 head cauliflower, cut into florets
- 1/2 cup of black olives, pitted and chopped
- 1 cup roasted bell peppers, chopped
- 1 red onion, sliced
- 1/2 cup cashew nuts
- Chopped celery leaves, for garnish
- 1/4 cup olive oil
- 1/3 tsp. salt
- 1/4 tsp. ground black pepper
- 1/4 tsp. mustard
- 2 tbsp. balsamic vinegar

Directions:

1. Add the cauliflower into a pot of boiling salted water. Allow to boil for 4 to 5 minutes until fork-tender but still crisp.
2. Remove from the heat & drain on paper towels, then transfer the cauliflower to a bowl.
3. Add the olives, bell pepper, and red onion. Stir well.
4. Make the dressing: In a separate bowl, mix the olive oil, mustard, vinegar, salt, and pepper. Pour the dressing over the veggies & toss to combine.
5. Serve topped with cashew nuts and celery leaves.

Nutrition for Total Servings:

- **Calories:** 298 Cal
- **Fat:** 20 g
- **Carbs:** 4 g
- **Protein:** 8 g
- **Fiber:** 3 g

Salmon and Lettuce Salad

Preparation time: 10 minutes
Cooking time: 0 minutes
Servings: 4
Ingredients:

- 1 tbsp. extra-virgin olive oil
- 2 slices smoked salmon, chopped
- 3 tbsps. mayonnaise
- 1 tbsp. lime juice
- Sea salt, to taste
- 1 cup romaine lettuce, shredded
- 1 tsp. onion flakes
- 1/2 avocado, sliced

Directions:

1. In a bowl, stir the olive oil, salmon, mayo, lime juice, and salt. Stir well until the salmon is coated fully.
2. Divide evenly the romaine lettuce and onion flakes among four serving plates. Spread the salmon mixture over the lettuce, then serve topped with avocado slices.

Nutrition for Total Servings:

- **Calories:** 271 Cal
- **Fat:** 18 g
- **Carbs:** 4 g
- **Protein:** 6 g

Prawns Salad with Mixed Lettuce Greens

Preparation time: 10 minutes
Cooking time: 3 minutes
Servings: 4
Ingredients:
- 1/2 pound (227 g) prawns, peeled and deveined
- Salt and chili pepper, to taste
- 1 tbsp. olive oil
- 2 cups mixed lettuce greens
- 1 tbsp. mustard
- 1 tbsp. lemon juice

Directions:
1. In a bowl, add the prawns, salt, and chili pepper. Toss well.
2. Warm the olive oil over medium heat. Add the seasoned prawns and fry for about 6 to 8 minutes, stirring occasionally, or until the prawns are opaque.
3. Remove from the heat and set the prawns aside on a platter.
4. Make the dressing: In a small bowl, mix the mustard, and lemon juice until creamy and smooth.
5. Make the salad: In a separate bowl, add the mixed lettuce greens. Pour the dressing over the greens and toss to combine.
6. Divide salad among 4 serving plates and serve it alongside the prawns.

Nutrition for Total Servings:
- **Calories:** 228 Cal
- **Fat:** 17 g
- **Carbs:** 3 g
- **Protein:** 5 g

Beef Salad with Vegetables

Preparation time: 10 minutes
Cooking time: 10 minutes
Servings: 4
Ingredients:

- 1-pound (454 g) ground beef
- 1/4 cup pork rinds, crushed
- 1 egg, whisked
- 1 onion, grated
- 1 tbsp. fresh parsley, chopped
- 1/2 tsp. dried oregano
- 1 garlic clove, minced
- Salt and black pepper, to taste
- 2 tbsps. olive oil, divided

Salad:

- 1 cup chopped arugula
- 1 cucumber, sliced
- 1 cup cherry tomatoes, halved
- 1 1/2 tbsps. lemon juice
- Salt and pepper, to taste

Directions:

1. Stir together the beef, pork rinds, whisked egg, onion, parsley, oregano, garlic, salt, and pepper in a large bowl until completely mixed.
2. Make the meatballs: On a lightly floured surface, using a cookie scoop to scoop out equal-sized amounts of the beef mixture and form into meatballs with your palm.
3. Heat 1 tbsp. olive oil in a large skillet over medium heat, fry the meatballs for about 4 minutes on each side until cooked through.
4. Remove from the heat & set aside on a plate to cool.
5. In a salad bowl, mix the arugula, cucumber, cherry tomatoes, 1 tbsp. olive oil, and lemon juice. Season with salt and pepper.
6. Make the dressing: In a third bowl, whisk the soy milk, yogurt, and mint until well blended. Pour the mixture over the salad. Serve topped with the meatballs.

Nutrition for Total Servings:

- **Calories:** 302 Cal
- **Fat:** 13 g
- **Carbs:** 6 g
- **Protein:** 7 g

Niçoise Salad

Preparation time: 5 minutes
Cooking time: 30 minutes
Servings: 6
Ingredients:
- 2 tbsps. butter
- 3 cups oil-packed tuna
- 2 ounces lettuce
- 1 cup green beans
- 3 anchovies packed in oil
- 2 avocado
- 1 cup diced tomatoes
- 1/2 cup of black olives

For the dressing:
- 3/4 cup MCT oil
- 1/2 cup lemon juice
- 1 tsp. Dijon mustard
- 1 tbsp. fresh thyme leaves, minced
- 1 medium shallot, minced
- 2 teaspoons fresh oregano leaves, minced
- 2 tbsps. fresh basil leaves, minced
- Celtic sea salt & freshly ground black pepper, to taste

Directions:
1. Melt the butter and heat the olive oil in a nonstick skillet over medium-high heat. Place tuna steaks in the skillet, and sear for 3 minutes or until opaque, flipping once. Set aside.
2. Make the dressing: Combine all the ingredients for the dressing in a bowl.
3. Make six niçoise salads: Dunk the lettuce and tuna steaks in the dressing bowl to coat well, then arrange the tuna in the middle of the lettuce. Set aside.
4. Blanch green beans in a pot of boiling salted water for 3 to 5 minutes or until soft but still crisp. Drain and dry with paper towels.
5. Dunk the green beans in the dressing bowl to coat well. Arrange them around the tuna steaks on the lettuce.
6. Top the tuna and green beans with hard-boiled eggs, anchovies, avocado chunks, tomatoes, and olives. Sprinkle 2 tbsps. Dressing over each egg, then serve.

Nutrition for Total Servings:
- **Calories:** 197 Cal
- **Fat:** 16 g
- **Carbs:** 8 g
- **Protein:** 6 g

Baked Carrot with Bacon

Preparation time: 10 minutes
Cooking time: 35 minutes
Servings: 4
Ingredients:
- 1 1/2 lb. carrots, peeled
- 12 slices bacon
- 1 tbsp. black pepper
- 1/3 cup maple syrup
- 1 pinch parsley

Directions:
1. Now, preheat the oven to 400°F.
2. Wrap the bacon slices around your carrots from top to bottom. Add black pepper, sprinkle with maple syrup, and bake for about 20-25 minutes.
3. Top with parsley and serve.

Nutrition for Total Servings:
- **Carbohydrates**: 16 g
- **Fat:** 26 g
- **Protein:** 10 g
- **Calories:** 421

Standard Greek Salad

Preparation time: 15 minutes
Cooking time: 0 minutes
Servings: 4
Ingredients:
- 1 large tomato, cut into cubes
- 1 cucumber, sliced into half-moons
- 1/3 cup kalamata olives, halved
- 1/2 white onion, sliced
- 3/4 cup feta, crumbled
- 2 tbsp. red wine vinegar
- 2 tbsp. lemon juice
- 1 tsp. oregano, dried
- Salt and pepper to taste
- 1/4 cup extra-virgin olive oil

Directions:
1. In separate bowl, combine the tomatoes, cucumbers, olives, and onion. Stir and top the mix with feta.
2. Another bowl, stir together the lemon juice, vinegar, oregano, salt, pepper, and olive oil. Gently whisk.
3. Sprinkle the salad with the dressing.

Nutrition for Total Servings:
- **Carbs:** 7 g
- **Fat:** 20 g
- **Protein:** 5 g
- **Calories:** 230

Creamy Mushrooms with Garlic and Thyme

Preparation time: 5 minutes
Cooking time: 15 minutes
Servings: 4
Ingredients:
- 1 lb. button mushrooms
- 2 tsp. garlic, diced
- 1 tbsp. fresh thyme
- 1 tbsp. parsley, chopped
- 1/2 tsp. salt
- 1/4 tsp. black pepper

Directions:
1. Melt the butter in a pan. Place the mushrooms into the pan. Add salt and pepper. Cook the mushroom mix for about 5 minutes until they're browned on both sides.
2. Add the garlic and thyme. Additionally, sauté the mushrooms for 1-2 minutes. Top them with parsley.

Nutrition for Total Servings:
- **Carbs**: 45 g
- **Fat:** 8 g
- **Protein:** 3 g
- **Calories:** 99

Easy Roasted Broccoli

Preparation time: 2 minutes
Cooking time: 19 minutes
Servings: 4
Ingredients:
- 1 lb. frozen broccoli, cut into florets
- 3 tsp. olive oil
- Sea salt to taste

Directions:
1. Place broccoli florets on a baking sheet greased with oil and put it in the oven (preheated to 400°F). Sprinkle the olive oil over the florets.
2. Cook for 12 minutes. Whisk well and bake for an additional 7 minutes.

Nutrition for Total Servings:
- **Carbs:** 8 g
- **Fat:** 3 g
- **Protein:** 3 g
- **Calories:** 58

Roasted Cabbage with Bacon

Preparation time: 10 minutes
Cooking time: 40 minutes
Servings: 4
Ingredients:
- 1/2 head cabbage, quartered
- 8 slices bacon, cut into thick pieces
- 1 tsp. garlic powder
- Salt and pepper to taste
- 1 pinch parsley, chopped

Directions:
1. Lightly sprinkle the cabbage wedges with the garlic powder. Wrap 2 pieces of bacon around each cabbage wedge.
2. Place your wrapped cabbage wedges on the baking sheet and put into the oven preheated to 350°F oven. Bake for 35-40 minutes. Top with parsley.

Nutrition for Total Servings:
- **Carbs:** 7 g
- **Fat:** 19 g
- **Protein:** 9 g
- **Calories:** 236

Baked Radish Snack

Preparation time: 8 minutes
Cooking time: 22 minutes
Servings: 2
Ingredients:

- 8 oz. red radishes, washed and trimmed
- 2 tbsp. olive oil
- 2 tbsp. unsalted butter
- 1 clove garlic, diced
- 1 tsp. lemon juice
- 1/4 tsp. oregano, dried
- Salt and pepper to taste

Directions:

1. Place the halved or quartered radishes into a separate bowl. Drizzle over the olive oil and add oregano. Stir gently.
2. Put the radish on the baking sheet and place it in the oven (preheated to 450°F).
3. Bake for 18-22 minutes. Mix a few times while baking.
4. Melt the butter in a saucepan. Add garlic and cook for about 3-5 minutes.
5. Remove your roasted radishes from the oven, sprinkle them with lemon juice, and top with the butter mix.

Nutrition for Total Servings:

- **Carbs:** 4 g
- **Fat:** 17 g
- **Protein:** 1 g
- **Calories:** 164

Boiled Asparagus with Sliced Lemon

Preparation time: 5 minutes
Cooking time: 7 minutes
Servings: 1
Ingredients:
- 10 large asparagus
- 3 tbsp. avocado oil
- 1/4 tbsp. lemon juice
- 2-3 pieces lemon
- 1/4 cup water
- 1/2 tsp. salt

Directions:
1. Place the asparagus in a pot of water. Boil for about 5-7 minutes.
2. Take the asparagus out of the pot. Sprinkle with lemon juice, avocado oil, and salt. Serve with the pieces of lemon.

Nutrition for Total Servings:
- **Carbs:** 10.7 g
- **Fat:** 43 g
- **Protein:** 4.7 g
- **Calories:** 447

Stuffed Eggs with Bacon-Avocado Filling

Preparation time: 10 minutes
Cooking time: 10 minutes
Servings: 1
Ingredients:

- 2 eggs, boiled and halved
- 1 tbsp. mayonnaise
- 1/4 tsp. mustard
- 1/8 Lemon, squeezed
- 1/4 tsp. garlic powder
- 1/8 Tsp. salt
- 1/4 avocado
- 16 small pieces of bacon

Directions:

1. Fry the bacon for 3 minutes in a pan. Add the avocado and fry for another 3 minutes (on lower heat).
2. Combine the mayonnaise, mustard, lemon, garlic powder, and salt in a separate bowl. Stir well.
3. Remove the yolk from the halved eggs and fill the egg halves with the mayonnaise mix. Top with the bacon-avocado filling.

Nutrition for Total Servings:

- **Carbs:** 4 g
- **Fat:** 30 g
- **Protein:** 16 g
- **Calories:** 342

Spinach

Preparation time: 5 minutes
Cooking time: 25 minutes
Servings: 8
Ingredients:

- 2 (10-ounce) packages of frozen spinach, thawed & drained
- 1 1/2 cups water, divided
- 1/4 cup sour cream
- Oat milk
- 2 tbsps. butter
- 1 tbsp. onion, minced
- 1 tbsp. garlic, minced
- 1 tbsp. fresh ginger, minced
- 2 tbsps. tomato puree
- 2 teaspoons curry powder
- 2 teaspoons garam masala powder
- 2 teaspoons ground coriander
- 2 teaspoons ground cumin
- 2 teaspoons ground turmeric
- 2 teaspoons red pepper flakes, crushed
- Salt, to taste

Directions:

1. Place spinach, 1/2 cup of water, and sour cream in a blender and pulse until pureed.
2. Transfer the spinach puree into a bowl and set aside.
3. In a large non-stick wok, melt butter over medium-low heat and sauté onion, garlic, ginger, tomato puree, spices, and salt for about 2–3 minutes.
4. Add the spinach puree and remaining water and stir to combine.
5. Adjust the heat to medium & cook for about 3–5 minutes.
6. Add oat milk and stir to combine.
7. Adjust heat to low & cook for about 10–15 minutes.

8. Serve hot.

Nutrition for Total Servings:
- **Calories**: 121 Cal
- **Fat**: 12 g
- **Carbs:** 9 g
- **Protein:** 4 g

CHAPTER 5:

Main Dishes

Cole Slaw Keto Wrap

Preparation time: 15 minutes.
Cooking time: 20 minutes.
Servings: 2
Ingredients:
- 3 cups sliced thin red cabbage
- 0.5 cups green onions, diced
- 0.75 cups mayo
- 2 teaspoons apple cider vinegar
- 0.25 teaspoon salt
- 16 pieces collard green, stems removed
- 1 pound ground meat of choice, cooked and chilled
- 0.33 cup alfalfa sprouts
- Toothpicks, to hold wraps together

Directions:
1. Mix the slaw ingredients with a spoon in a large-sized bowl until everything is well-coated.
2. Place a collard green on a plate and scoop a tablespoon or two of coleslaw on the edge of the leaf. Top it with a scoop of meat and sprouts.
3. Roll and tuck the sides to keep the filling from spilling.
4. Once you assemble the wrap, put in your toothpicks in a way that holds the wrap together until you are ready to beat it. Just repeat this with the leftover leaves.

Nutrition:
- **Calories:** 409
- **Carbs:** 4g
- **Fat:** 42g
- **Protein:** 2g

Keto Chicken Club Lettuce Wrap

Preparation time: 15 minutes.
Cooking time: 15 minutes.
Servings: 1
Ingredients:

- 1 head of iceberg lettuce with the core and outer leaves removed
- 1 tablespoon mayonnaise
- 6 slices of organic chicken or turkey breast
- 2 cooked strips bacon, halved
- 2 slices of tomato

Directions:

1. Line your working surface with a large slice of parchment paper.
2. Layer 6–8 large leaves of lettuce in the center of the paper to make a base of around 9–10 inches.
3. Spread the mayo in the center and lay with chicken or turkey, bacon, and tomato.
4. Starting with the end closest to you, roll the wrap like a jelly roll with the parchment paper as your guide. Keep it tight and halfway through, roll tuck in the ends of the wrap.
5. When it is completely wrapped, roll the rest of the parchment paper around it, and use a knife to cut it in half.

Nutrition:

- **Carbs:** 4g
- **Fat:** 78g
- **Protein:** 28g
- **Calories:** 837

Keto Broccoli Salad

Preparation time: 10 minutes.
Cooking time: 0 minutes.
Servings: 4–6
Ingredients:
For your salad:
- 2 medium-sized heads broccoli, florets chunked
- 2 cups red cabbage, well shredded
- 0.5 cups sliced almonds, roasted
- 1 stalk green onions, sliced
- 0.5 cups raisins

For your orange almond dressing:
- 0.33 cup orange juice
- 0.25 cup almond butter
- 2 tablespoons coconut aminos
- 1 shallot, small-sized, chopped finely
- ½ teaspoon salt

Directions:
1. Use a food processor to pulse together salt, shallot, amino, nut butter, and orange juice. Make sure it is perfectly smooth.
2. Use a medium-sized bowl to combine the other ingredients. Toss it with dressing and serve.

Nutrition:
- **Carbs:** 13g
- **Fat:** 94g
- **Protein:** 22g
- **Calories:** 1022

Keto Sheet Pan Chicken and Rainbow Veggies

Preparation time: 15 minutes.
Cooking time: 25 minutes.
Servings: 4
Ingredients:
- Nonstick spray
- 1 pound chicken breasts, boneless, and skinless
- 1 tablespoon sesame oil
- 2 tablespoons soy sauce
- 2 tablespoons honey
- 2 red pepper, medium-sized, sliced
- 2 yellow pepper, medium-sized, sliced
- 3 carrots, medium-sized, sliced
- ½ head broccoli cut up
- 2 red onions, medium-size and sliced
- 2 tablespoons EVOO
- Pepper and salt, to taste
- 0.25 cup parsley, fresh herb, chopped

Directions:
1. First, spray your baking sheet with cooking spray and bring the oven to a temperature of 400°F.
2. Then, put the chicken in the middle of the sheet. Separately, combine the oil and the soy sauce. Brush the mix over the chicken.
3. Separate your veggies across the plate. Sprinkle with oil and then toss them gently to ensure they are coated. Finally, spice up with pepper and salt.
4. Set tray into the oven and cook for around 25 minutes until all is tender and done throughout.
5. After taking it out of the oven, garnish using parsley. Divide everything between those prepared containers paired with your favorite greens.

Nutrition:
- **Carbs:** 9g
- **Fat:** 30g
- **Protein:** 30g
- **Calories:** 437kcal

Skinny Bang Bang Zucchini Noodles

Preparation time: 15 minutes.
Cooking time: 15 minutes.
Servings: 4
Ingredients:
For the noodles:

- 4 medium zucchini spiraled
- 1 tablespoon olive oil

For the sauce:

- 0.25 cup + 2 tablespoons plain Greek yogurt
- 0.25 cup + 2 tablespoons mayo
- 0.25 cup + 2 tablespoons Thai sweet chili sauce
- 1.5 teaspoons honey
- 1.5 teaspoons sriracha
- 2 teaspoons lime juice

Directions:

1. If you are using any meats for this dish, such as chicken or shrimp, cook them first, then set them aside.
2. Pour the oil into a large-sized skillet at medium temperature.
3. After the oil is well heated, stir in the spiraled zucchini noodles.
4. Cook the "noodles" until tender yet still crispy.
5. Remove from the heat, drain, and set at rest for at least 10 minutes.
6. Combine the sauce ingredients together into a large-sized, both until perfectly smooth.
7. Give it a taste and adjust as needed.
8. Divide into 4 small containers. Mix your noodles with any meats you cooked and add them to meal prepared containers.
9. When you're ready to eat it, heat the noodles, drain any excess water, and mix in the sauce.

Nutrition:

- **Carbs:** 18g
- **Fat:** 1g
- **Protein**: 9g
- **Calories:** 161g

Keto Caesar Salad

Preparation time: 15 minutes.
Cooking time: 0 minutes.
Servings: 4
Ingredients:

- 1.5 cups mayonnaise
- 3 tablespoons apple cider vinegar/ACV
- 1 teaspoon Dijon mustard
- 4 anchovy fillets
- 24 romaine heart leaves
- 4 ounces pork rinds, chopped

Directions:

1. Place the mayo with ACV, mustard, and anchovies into a blender and process until smooth and dressing like.
2. Prepare romaine leaves and pour out dressing across them evenly.
3. Top with pork rinds and enjoy.

Nutrition:

- **Carbs:** 4g
- **Fat:** 86g
- **Protein:** 47g
- **Calories:** 993kcal

Keto Buffalo Chicken Empanadas

Preparation time: 20 minutes.
Cooking time: 30 minutes.
Servings: 6
Ingredients:
For the empanada dough:

- 1(½) cups mozzarella cheese
- 3 ounces cream cheese
- 1 whisked egg
- 2 cups almond flour

For the buffalo chicken filling:

- 2 cups of cooked shredded chicken
- 2 tablespoons butter, melted
- 0.33 cup hot sauce

Directions:

1. Bring the oven to a temperature of 425°F.
2. Put the cheese and cream cheese into a microwave-safe dish. Microwave at 1-minute intervals until completely combined.
3. Stir the flour and egg into the dish until it is well-combined. Add any additional flour for consistency—until it stops sticking to your fingers.
4. With another medium-sized bowl, combine the chicken with sauce and set aside.
5. Cover a flat surface with plastic wrap or parchment paper and sprinkle with almond flour.
6. Spray a rolling pin to avoid sticking and use it to press the dough flat.
7. Make circle shapes out of this dough with a lid, a cup, or a cookie-cutter. For the excess dough, roll back up and repeat the process.
8. Portion out spoonful of filling into these dough circles but keep them only on one half.
9. Fold the other half over to close up into half-moon shapes. Press on the edges to seal them.
10. Lay on a lightly greased cooking sheet and bake for around 9 minutes until perfectly brown.

Nutrition:

- **Carbs:** 20g
- **Fat:** 96g
- **Protein:** 74g
- **Calories:** 1217kcal

Pepperoni and Cheddar Stromboli

Preparation time: 15 minutes.
Cooking time: 20 minutes.
Servings: 3
Ingredients:

- 1.25 cups mozzarella cheese
- 0.25 cup almond flour
- 3 tablespoons coconut flour
- 1 teaspoon Italian seasoning
- 1 large-sized egg, whisked
- 6 ounces deli ham, sliced
- 2 ounces pepperoni, sliced
- 4 ounces cheddar cheese, sliced
- 1 tablespoon butter, melted
- 6 cups salad greens

Directions:

1. First, bring the oven to a temperature of 400°F and prepare a baking tray with some parchment paper.
2. Use the microwave to melt the mozzarella until it can be stirred.
3. Mix flours and Italian seasoning in a separate small-sized bowl.
4. Put the melted cheese and stir together with pepper and salt to taste.
5. Stir in the egg and process the dough with your hands. Pour it onto that prepared baking tray.
6. Roll out the dough with your hands or a pin. Cut slits that mark out 4 equal rectangles.
7. Put the ham and cheese onto the dough, then brush with butter and close up, putting the seal end down.
8. Bake for around 17 minutes until well-browned. Slice up and serve.

Nutrition:

- **Carbs:** 20g
- **Fat:** 13g
- **Protein:** 11g
- **Calories:** 240kcal

Tuna Casserole

Preparation time: 15 minutes.
Cooking time: 10 minutes.
Servings: 4
Ingredients:
- 16 ounces tuna in oil, drained
- 2 tablespoons butter
- 1(1/2) teaspoon salt
- 1 teaspoon black pepper
- 1 teaspoon chili powder
- 6 stalks celery
- 1 teaspoon green bell pepper
- 1 teaspoon yellow onion
- 4 ounces Parmesan cheese, grated
- 1 cup mayonnaise

Directions:
1. Heat the oven to 400°F.
2. Chop the onion, bell pepper, and celery very fine and fry in the melted butter for five minutes.
3. Stir together with the chili powder, parmesan cheese, tuna, and mayonnaise.
4. Use lard to grease an eight by eight-inch or nine by a nine-inch baking pan.
5. Add the tuna mixture into the fried vegetables and spoon the mix into the baking pan.
6. Bake it for twenty minutes.

Nutrition:
- **Calories:** 953
- **Carbs:** 5g
- **Fat:** 83g
- **Protein:** 43g

Brussels Sprout and Hamburger Gratin

Preparation time: 15 minutes.
Cooking time: 20 minutes.
Servings: 4
Ingredients:

- 1 pound ground beef
- 8 ounces bacon, diced small
- 15 ounces Brussels sprouts, cut in half
- 1 teaspoon salt
- 1 teaspoon black pepper
- 1(1/2) teaspoon thyme
- 1 cup Cheddar cheese, shredded
- 1 tablespoon Italian seasoning
- 4 tablespoons sour cream
- 2 tablespoons butter

Directions:

1. Heat the oven to 425°F.
2. Fry bacon and Brussels sprouts in butter for five minutes.
3. Stir in the sour cream and pour this mix into a greased eight by and eight-inch baking pan.
4. Cook the ground beef and season with salt and pepper, then add this mix to the baking pan.
5. Top with the herbs and the shredded cheese. Bake for twenty minutes.

Nutrition:

- **Calories:** 770kcal
- **Carbs:** 8g
- **Fat:** 62g
- **Protein:** 42g

Bacon Appetizers

Preparation time: 15 minutes.
Cooking time: 2 hours.
Servings: 6
Ingredients:
- 1 pack Keto crackers
- ¾ cup Parmesan cheese, grated
- 1 pound bacon, sliced thinly

Directions:
1. Preheat your oven to 250°F.
2. Arrange the crackers on a baking sheet.
3. Sprinkle cheese on top of each cracker.
4. Wrap each cracker with the bacon.
5. Bake in the oven for 2 hours.

Nutrition:
- **Calories:** 290kcal
- **Protein:** 11.66g
- **Fat:** 25.94g
- **Carbs:** 6.84g

Cherry Tomato Salad with Chorizo

Preparation time: 15 minutes.
Cooking time: 50 minutes.
Servings: 4
Ingredients:

- 2.5 cups cherry tomatoes
- 4 chorizo sausages
- 2.5 tablespoons olive oil
- 2 teaspoons red wine vinegar
- 1 small red onion
- 2 tablespoons cilantro
- 2 ounces Kalamata olives
- Black pepper and salt

Directions:

1. Chop the onions and sausage. Slice the olives and onions into halves, and set aside.
2. Heat a skillet and add one tablespoon of oil to cook the chorizo until browned.
3. Prepare a salad dish with the rest of the oil, vinegar, onion, tomatoes, chorizo, and cilantro.
4. Toss thoroughly and sprinkle with salt, pepper, and olives.

Nutrition:

- **Calories:** 138
- **Net carbohydrates:** 5.2g
- **Protein:** 7g
- **Fat content:** 8.9g

Chicken Caesar Salad & Bok Choy

Preparation time: 10 minutes.
Cooking time: 40 minutes
Servings: 4
Ingredients:
- 4 Chicken thighs—no skin or bones
- 0.25 cups lemon juice
- 4 tablespoons olive oil
- 0.5 cup Caesar salad dressing—keto-friendly
- 12 bok choy
- 3 Parmesan crisps
- To Garnish: Parmesan cheese

Directions:
1. Prepare the bok choy in lengthwise pieces.
2. Add these ingredients to a zipper-type plastic bag; two tablespoons of oil, lemon juice, and chicken. Seal and shake the bag. Pop it in the fridge to marinate for about one hour.
3. Prepare a grill using the medium temperature setting and cook the chicken for four minutes on each side.
4. Brush the bok Choy with the rest of the oil to grill for three minutes.
5. Place the bok choy on the serving dish topped with the chicken and a spritz of dressing, cheese, and parmesan crisps.

Nutrition:
- **Calories:** 529
- **Carbs:** 5g
- **Protein:** 33g
- **Fat:** 39g

Healthy Roasted Green Bean & Mushroom Salad

Preparation time: 10 minutes.
Cooking time: 30 minutes
Servings provided: 4
Ingredients:

- 0.5 cup green beans
- 1 pound sliced Cremini mushrooms
- 3 tablespoons vegan melted butter
- 1 lemon, for juice
- 4 tablespoons toasted hazelnuts
- 2 tablespoons Butter
- 1 tablespoon Salt
- 1 tablespoon Pepper

Directions:

1. Set the oven to 450°F. Slice and add the mushrooms and green beans to a baking dish.
2. Drizzle them with butter, salt, and pepper.
3. Set the timer and roast them for 20 minutes.
4. Place the veggies in a salad dish with a spritz of lemon juice and a hazelnuts' sprinkle to serve.

Nutrition:

- **Calories:** 179
- **Carbs:** 7g
- **Protein:** 5g
- **Fat:** 11g

Italian Tri-Color Salad

Preparation time: 10 minutes.
Cooking time: 40 minutes.
Servings Provided: 4
Ingredients:

- 0.25 pounds buffalo mozzarella cheese
- 1 avocado
- 3 tomatoes
- 8 Kalamata olives
- 2 tablespoons pesto sauce
- 2 tablespoons olive oil

Directions:

1. Slice the tomatoes, avocado, and mozzarella.
2. Stack the tomatoes on a serving platter.
3. Arrange them with the sliced tomatoes, avocado in the center with olives all over it.
4. Drop the pieces of cheese over the salad and serve with a drizzle of oil and pesto sauce.

Nutrition:

- **Calories:** 290
- **Carbs:** 4.3g
- **Protein:** 9g
- **Fat:** 25g

Lemon-Garlic Chicken Thighs

Preparation time: 10 minutes.
Cooking time: 25 minutes.
Servings: 4
Ingredients

- 4 wedges lemon
- ¼ cup lemon juice
- 4 chicken thighs
- 2 tablespoon olive oil
- Pinch ground black pepper
- 1 teaspoon Dijon mustard
- ¼ teaspoon salt
- 2 garlic cloves, thinly cut

Directions

1. Before anything, ensure that your air fryer is preheated 360°F.
2. Into a medium-sized bowl, add lemon juice, pepper, salt, olive oil, garlic, and Dijon mustard. Using a whisk, combine these ingredients and set them aside for a bit. This is your marinade.
3. You'll need a large reusable bag for this part. Put your chicken thighs and the marinade inside the bag and seal it. Leave it in your refrigerator for about 2 hours.
4. Next, take the chicken thighs out of the reusable bag, and using a paper towel, dry out the marinade. Place the thighs in an air fryer basket and cook them. You could fry them in batches, if that made it easier.
5. When the chicken thighs no longer look pink close to the bone, the frying should last up to 24 minutes to achieve this, you can take them out of the air fryer. If you place an instant-read thermometer on the bone, it should read 165°F.
6. When you serve the chicken thighs, also squeeze the lemon wedges on each of them.

Nutrition:

- **Calories:** 258
- **Carbs:** 3.6g
- **Protein:** 19.4g
- **Fat:** 6g

Black-Eyed Peas Platter

Preparation time: 10 minutes.
Cooking time: 8 hours.
Servings: 4
Ingredients:

- 1 cup black eyed-peas, soaked overnight and drained
- 2 cups low-sodium vegetable broth
- 1 can (15 ounces) tomatoes, diced with juice
- 8 ounces ham, chopped
- 1 onion, chopped
- 2 garlic cloves, minced
- 1 teaspoon dried oregano
- 1 teaspoon salt
- ½ teaspoon freshly ground black pepper
- ½ teaspoon ground mustard
- 1 bay leaf

Directions:

1. Add the listed ingredients to your Slow Cooker and stir.
2. Place lid and cook over low heat for 8 hours.
3. Discard the bay leaf.
4. Serve and enjoy!

Nutrition:

- **Calories:** 209
- **Carbs:** 17g
- **Protein:** 27g
- **Fat:** 6g

Humble Mushroom Rice

Preparation time: 10 minutes.
Cooking time: 3 hours.
Servings: 3
Ingredients:

- ½ cup rice
- 2 green onions chopped
- 1 garlic clove, minced
- ¼ pound baby Portobello mushrooms, sliced
- 1 cup vegetable stock

Directions:

1. Add rice, onions, garlic, mushrooms, and stock to your slow cooker.
2. Stir well and place the lid.
3. Cook over low heat for 3 hours.
4. Stir and divide amongst serving platters.
5. Enjoy!

Nutrition:

- **Calories:** 200
- **Carbs:** 12g
- **Protein:** 28g
- **Fat:** 6g

Sweet and Sour Cabbage and Apples

Preparation time: 15 minutes.
Cooking time: 8 hours and 15 minutes.
Servings: 4
Ingredients:

- ¼ cup honey
- ¼ cup apple cider vinegar
- 2 tablespoons orange chili-garlic sauce
- 1 teaspoon sea salt
- 3 sweet-tart apples, peeled, cored and sliced
- 2 heads green cabbage, cored and shredded
- 1 sweet red onion, thinly sliced

Directions:

1. Take a small bowl and whisk in honey, orange-chili garlic sauce, vinegar.
2. Stir well.
3. Add the honey mix, apples, onion, and cabbage to your slow cooker and stir.
4. Close the lid and cook over low heat for 8 hours.
5. Serve and enjoy!

Nutrition:

- **Calories:** 164
- **Carbs:** 41g
- **Protein:** 24g
- **Fat:** 2.5g

Orange and Chili Garlic Sauce

Preparation time: 15 minutes.
Cooking time: 8 hours and 15 minutes.
Servings: 5
Ingredients:

- ½ cup apple cider vinegar
- 4 pounds red jalapeno peppers, stems, seeds, and ribs removed, chopped
- 10 garlic cloves, chopped
- ½ cup tomato paste
- Juice of 1 orange zest
- ½ cup honey
- 2 tablespoons soy sauce
- 2 teaspoons salt

Directions:

1. Add vinegar, garlic, peppers, tomato paste, orange juice, honey, zest, soy sauce, and salt to your slow cooker.
2. Stir and close the lid.
3. Cook over low heat for 8 hours.
4. Use as needed!

Nutrition:

- **Calories:** 33
- **Carbs:** 8g
- **Protein:** 12g
- **Fat:** 4g

Tantalizing Mushroom Gravy

Preparation time: 5 minutes.
Cooking time: 5–8 hours.
Servings: 2
Ingredients:

- 1/3 cup water
- 1 cup button mushrooms, sliced
- ¾ cup low-fat buttermilk
- 1 medium onion, finely diced
- 2 garlic cloves, minced
- 2 tablespoons extra virgin olive oil
- 2 tablespoons all-purpose flour
- 1 tablespoon fresh rosemary, minced
- Freshly ground black pepper

Directions:

1. Add the listed ingredients to your slow cooker. Place the lid and cook over low heat for 5–8 hours.
2. Serve warm and use as needed!

Nutrition:

- **Calories:** 190
- **Carbs:** 4g
- **Protein:** 2g
- **Fat:** 6g

Everyday Vegetable Stock

Preparation time: 5 minutes.
Cooking time: 8-12 hours.
Servings: 4
Ingredients:

- 2 celery stalks (with leaves), quartered
- 4 ounces mushrooms, with stems
- 2 carrots, unpeeled and quartered
- 1 onion, unpeeled, quartered from pole to pole
- 1 garlic head, unpeeled, halved across the middle
- 2 fresh thyme sprigs
- 10 peppercorns
- ½ teaspoon salt
- Enough water to fill 3 quarters of slow cooker

Directions:

1. Add celery, mushrooms, onion, carrots, garlic, thyme, salt, peppercorn, and water to your slow cooker.
2. Stir and cover.
3. Cook over low heat for 8–12 hours.
4. Strain the stock through a fine–mesh cloth/metal mesh and discard solids.
5. Use as needed.

Nutrition:

- **Calories:** 38
- **Carbs:** 1g
- **Protein:** 0g
- **Fat:** 1.2g

Grilled Chicken with Lemon and Fennel

Preparation time: 5 minutes.
Cooking time: 25 minutes.
Servings: 5
Ingredients:
- 2 cups chicken fillets, cut and skewed
- 1 large fennel bulb
- 2 garlic cloves
- 1 jar green olives
- 1 lemon

Directions:
1. Preheat your grill to medium-high.
2. Crush garlic cloves.
3. Take a bowl and add olive oil and season with sunflower seeds and pepper.
4. Coat chicken skewers with the marinade.
5. Transfer them under the grill and grill for 20 minutes, making sure to turn them halfway through until golden.
6. Zest half of the lemon and cut the other half into quarters.
7. Cut the fennel bulb into similarly sized segments.
8. Brush olive oil all over the garlic clove segments and cook for 3–5 minutes.
9. Chop them and add them to the bowl with the marinade.
10. Add lemon zest and olives.
11. Once the meat is ready, serve with the vegetable mix.
12. Enjoy!

Nutrition:
- **Calories:** 649
- **Carbs:** 15g
- **Protein:** 28g
- **Fat:** 6g

Caramelized Pork Chops and Onion

Preparation time: 5 minutes.
Cooking time: 40 minutes.
Servings: 4
Ingredients:

- 4-pound chuck roast
- 2 medium sized Onions
- 1 tablespoon Pepper
- 1 tablespoon of Sunflower seeds
- 2 tablespoons Oil

Directions:

1. Rub the chops with a seasoning of 1 teaspoon of pepper and 2 teaspoons of sunflower seeds.
2. Take a skillet and place it over medium heat, add oil and allow the oil to heat up
3. Brown the seasoned chop on both sides. Add water and onion to the skillet and cover, lower the heat to low, and simmer for 20 minutes. Turn the chops over and season with more sunflower seeds and pepper. Cover and cook until the water fully evaporates and the beer shows a slightly brown texture.
4. Remove the chops and serve with a topping of the caramelized onion.
5. Serve and enjoy!

Nutrition:

- **Calories:** 47
- **Carbs:** 4g
- **Protein:** 0.5g
- **Fat:** 4g

Hearty Pork Belly Casserole

Preparation time: 5 minutes.
Cooking time: 25 minutes.
Servings: 4
Ingredients:

- 8 pork belly slices, cut into small pieces
- 3 large onions, chopped
- 4 tablespoons lemon zest
- 2 tablespoons Honey
- 1 ounce parsley

Directions:

1. Take a large pressure cooker and place it over medium heat.
2. Add onions and sweat them for 5 minutes.
3. Add pork belly slices and cook until the meat browns and onions become golden.
4. Cover with water and add honey, lemon zest, sunflower seeds, pepper, and close the pressure seal.
5. Pressure cook for 40 minutes.
6. Serve and enjoy with a garnish of fresh chopped parsley if you prefer.

Nutrition:

- **Calories:** 753
- **Carbs:** 23g
- **Protein:** 36g
- **Fat:** 4g

Fascinating Spinach and Beef Meatballs

Preparation time: 10 minutes.
Cooking time: 20 minutes.
Servings: 4
Ingredients:

- ½ cup onion
- 4 garlic cloves
- 1 whole egg
- ¼ teaspoon oregano
- Pepper as needed
- 1 pound lean ground beef
- 10 ounces spinach

Directions:

1. Preheat your oven to 375°F.
2. Take a bowl and mix all the ingredients, and using your hands, roll into meatballs.
3. Transfer to a sheet tray and bake for 20 minutes.
4. Enjoy!

Nutrition:

- **Calories:** 200
- **Carbs:** 5g
- **Protein:** 29g
- **Fat:** 3g

Juicy and Peppery Tenderloin

Preparation time: 10 minutes.
Cooking time: 20 minutes.
Servings: 4
Ingredients:

- 2 teaspoons sage, chopped
- Sunflower seeds and pepper
- 2 1/2 pounds beef tenderloin
- 2 teaspoons thyme, chopped
- 2 garlic cloves, sliced
- 2 teaspoons rosemary, chopped
- 4 teaspoons olive oil

Directions:

1. Preheat your oven to 425°F.
2. Take a small knife and cut incisions in the tenderloin; insert one slice of garlic into the incision.
3. Rub meat with oil.
4. Take a bowl and add sunflower seeds, sage, thyme, rosemary, pepper, and mix well.
5. Rub the spice mix over the tenderloin.
6. Put rubbed tenderloin into the roasting pan and bake for 10 minutes.
7. Lower temperature to 350°F and cook for 20 minutes more until an internal thermometer reads 145°F.
8. Transfer tenderloin to a cutting board and let sit for 15 minutes; slice into 20 pieces and enjoy!

Nutrition:

- **Calories:** 490
- **Carbs:** 1g
- **Protein:** 24g
- **Fat:** 9g

Healthy Avocado Beef Patties

Preparation time: 15 minutes.
Cooking time: 10 minutes.
Servings: 2
Ingredients:
- 1 pound 85% lean ground beef
- 1 small avocado, pitted and peeled
- Fresh ground black pepper as needed

Directions:
1. Preheat and prepare your broiler to high.
2. Divide beef into two equal-sized patties.
3. Season the patties with pepper accordingly.
4. Broil the patties for 5 minutes per side.
5. Transfer the patties to a platter.
6. Slice avocado into strips and place them on top of the patties.
7. Serve and enjoy!

Nutrition:
- **Calories:** 560
- **Carbs:** 9g
- **Protein:** 38g
- **Fat:** 16g

Ravaging Beef Pot Roast

Preparation time: 10 minutes.
Cooking time: 1 hour and 15 minutes.
Servings: 4
Ingredients:

- 3(½) pounds beef roast
- 4 ounces mushrooms, sliced
- 12 ounces beef stock
- 1-ounce onion soup mix
- ½ cup Italian dressing, low sodium, and low fat

Directions:

1. Take a bowl and add the stock, onion soup mix, and Italian dressing.
2. Stir.
3. Put beef roast in a pan.
4. Add mushrooms, stock mix to the pan, and cover with foil.
5. Preheat your oven to 300°F.
6. Bake for 1 hour and 15 minutes.
7. Let the roast cool.
8. Slice and serve.
9. Enjoy with the gravy on top!

Nutrition:

- **Calories:** 700
- **Carbs:** 10g
- **Protein:** 46g
- **Fat:** 3g

Lovely Faux Mac and Cheese

Preparation time: 15 minutes.
Cooking time: 45 minutes.
Servings: 4
Ingredients:

- 5 cups cauliflower florets
- Sunflower seeds and pepper to taste
- 1 cup coconut almond milk
- ½ cup vegetable broth
- 2 tablespoons coconut flour, sifted
- 1 organic egg, beaten
- 1 cup cashew cheese

Directions:

1. Preheat your oven to 350°F.
2. Season florets with sunflower seeds and steam until firm.
3. Place florets in a greased ovenproof dish.
4. Heat coconut almond milk over medium heat in a skillet; make sure to season the oil with sunflower seeds and pepper.
5. Stir in broth and add coconut flour to the mix, stir.
6. Cook until the sauce begins to bubble.
7. Remove heat and add beaten egg.
8. Pour the thick sauce over the cauliflower and mix in cheese.
9. Bake for 30–45 minutes.
10. Serve and enjoy!

Nutrition:

- **Calories:** 229
- **Carbs:** 9g
- **Protein:** 15g
- **Fat:** 6g

Ancho Macho Chili

Preparation time: 20 minutes.
Cooking time: 1 hour and 30 minutes.
Servings: 4
Ingredients:

- 2 pounds lean sirloin
- 1 teaspoon salt
- 0.25 teaspoon pepper
- 1.5 tablespoons olive oil
- 0.5 medium-sized onion, chopped finely
- 1.5 tablespoons chili powder
- 7 ounces of can tomatoes with green chili
- ½ cup of chicken broth
- 2 cloves of large roasted and minced garlic

Directions:

1. Prepare the oven by bringing it to a temperature of 350F.
2. Coat prepared beef with pepper and salt.
3. Grab your Dutch oven cooker and bring a teaspoon of oil to a high temperature. Once it's ready, add in a third of your beef and cook until each side turns brown. Continue this process until all beef is brownish. Add more oil if needed.
4. Have about 1 teaspoon of oil left. Put that into the Dutch oven and use it for cooking your onion for a few minutes. Next, add in the last four ingredients and allow it to simmer in the pot.
5. Add in your beef with all its juices, cover the Dutch oven, and cook a full two hours. After the 1-hour point, stir everything. Enjoy!

Note: This recipe makes 4 servings and is good for 4–5 days. This can also be frozen.
Nutrition:

- **Carbs:** 6g
- **Fat:** 40g
- **Protein:** 58g
- **Calories:** 644kcal

Chicken Supreme Pizza

Preparation time: 25 minutes
Cooking time: 30 minutes
Servings: 4-8
Ingredients:

- 5 ounces of cooked and diced chicken breast
- 1.5 cups almond flour
- 1 teaspoon baking powder
- 1/2 teaspoon salt
- 0.25 cup water
- 1 red onion, small-sized, sliced thinly
- 1 red pepper, small-sized, sliced thinly
- Green pepper, same as red pepper above
- 1 cup mozzarella cheese, shredded
- 3 tablespoons olive oil

Directions:

1. Heat your oven to a temperature of 400°F.
2. Using a small-sized bowl and a fork, blend the flour together with the salt and baking powder.
3. Prepare your dough with the water and the oil added to this flour mixture. Prepare a space on your counter to make the dough flattened. Do what you need, but make sure the olive oil coats the surface lightly before you dump out the dough.
4. Dump out the dough. Use a rolling pin to press it out, and coat the pan with oil to avoid sticking. Once you archive the desired pizza crust shape, place it onto a baking stone or prepared tray.
5. Set the tray in the oven, and bake for about 12 minutes.
6. After taking out the pizza from the oven, sprinkle cheese onto it and then add chicken, pepper, and onion. Finally, season with pepper and salt (to taste).
7. Put the pizza back in the oven for only 15 minutes; serve warm and in slices.

Note: This recipe makes 4–8 servings depending on how you divide the pizza. This will keep for 3–4 days.

Nutrition:

- **Carbs:** 4g
- **Fat:** 12g
- **Protein:** 16g
- **Calories:** 310kcal

Zucchini Pizza Bites

Preparation time: 10 minutes.
Cooking time: 30 minutes.
Servings: 4
Ingredients:

- 4 large zucchinis
- 1 cup of tomato sauce
- 2 teaspoon oregano
- 4 cups mozzarella cheese
- 1/2 cup parmesan cheese
- Low carb pizza toppings of your choice

Directions:

1. Slice your zucchinis into small pieces, in a quarter of an inch or less.
2. Preheat the oven to 450°F.
3. Line a baking pan or tray with foil set it aside.
4. Place zucchini pieces on the pan. Top them with tomato sauce, cheese, oregano, and other low carb toppings you like.
5. Bake for five minutes, and then broil for five minutes more.
6. Serve warm.

Nutrition:

- **Calories:** 231
- **Protein:** 26.7g
- **Carbs:** 4.8g
- **Fat:** 74g

Pork Cutlets with Spanish Onion

Preparation time: 15 minutes
Cooking time: 15 minutes
Servings: 4
Ingredients:

- 1 tbsp. olive oil
- 2 pork cutlets
- 1 bell pepper, deveined and sliced
- 1 Spanish onion, chopped
- 2 garlic cloves, minced
- 1/2 tsp. hot sauce
- 1/2 tsp. mustard
- 1/2 tsp. paprika

Kitchen Equipment:

- Saucepan

Directions:

1. Fry the pork cutlets for 3 to 4 minutes until evenly golden and crispy on both sides.
2. Set the temperature to medium and add the bell pepper, Spanish onion, garlic, hot sauce, and mustard; continue cooking until the vegetables have softened, for a further 3 minutes.
3. Sprinkle with paprika, salt, and black pepper.
4. Serve immediately and enjoy!

Nutrition for Total Servings:

- **Calories:** 403
- **Protein:** 18.28 g
- **Fat:** 24.1g
- **Carbs:** 3.4g

Rich and Easy Pork Ragout

Preparation time: 15 minutes
Cooking time: 15 minutes
Servings: 4
Ingredients:
- 1 tsp. lard, melted at room temperature
- 3/4-pound pork butt, cut into bite-sized cubes
- 1 red bell pepper, deveined and chopped
- 1 poblano pepper, deveined and chopped
- 2 cloves garlic, pressed
- 1/2 cup leeks, chopped
- 1/2 tsp. mustard seeds
- 1/4 tsp. ground allspice
- 1/4 tsp. celery seeds
- 1 cup roasted vegetable broth
- 2 vine-ripe tomatoes, pureed

Kitchen Equipment:
- Stockpot

Directions:
1. Melt the lard in a stockpot over moderate heat. Once hot, cook the pork cubes for 4 to 6 minutes, occasionally stirring to ensure even cooking.
2. Then, stir in the vegetables and continue cooking until they are tender and fragrant. Add in the salt, pepper, mustard seeds, allspice, celery seeds, roasted vegetable broth, and tomatoes.
3. Reduce the heat to simmer. Let it simmer for 30 minutes longer or until everything is heated through. Ladle into individual bowls and serve hot. Bon appétit!

Nutrition for Total Servings:
- **Calories:** 389
- **Protein:** 23.17 g
- **Fat:** 24.3g
- **Carbs:** 5.4g

Pulled Pork with Mint

Preparation time: 20 minutes
Cooking time: 15 minutes
Servings: 2
Ingredients:
- 1 tsp. lard, melted at room temperature
- 3/4 pork Boston butt, sliced
- 2 garlic cloves, pressed
- 1/2 tsp. red pepper flakes, crushed
- 1/2 tsp. black peppercorns, freshly cracked
- Sea salt, to taste
- 2 bell peppers, deveined and sliced

Kitchen Equipment:
- Cast-iron skillet

Directions:
2. Melt the lard in a cast-iron skillet over a moderate flame. Once hot, brown the pork for 2 minutes per side until caramelized and crispy on the edges.
3. Set the temperature to medium-low and continue cooking for another 4 minutes, turning over periodically. Shred the pork with two forks and return to the skillet.
4. Add the garlic, red pepper, black peppercorns, salt, and bell pepper and continue cooking for a further 2 minutes or until the peppers are just tender and fragrant.

Nutrition for Total Servings:
- **Carbs:** 6.42 g
- **Calories:**370
- **Fat:** 21.9g
- **Protein:** 34.9g

Festive Meatloaf

Preparation time: 1 hour
Cooking time: 50 minutes
Servings: 2
Ingredients:

- 1/4-pound ground pork
- 1/2-pound ground chuck
- 2 eggs, beaten
- 1/4 cup flaxseed meal
- 1 shallot, chopped
- 2 garlic cloves, minced
- 1/2 tsp. smoked paprika
- 1/4 tsp. dried basil
- 1/4 tsp. ground cumin
- Kosher salt, to taste
- 1/2 cup tomato puree
- 1 tsp. mustard
- 1 tsp. liquid monk fruit

Kitchen Equipment:

- 2 mixing bowl
- Loaf pan
- Oven

Directions:

1. In a bowl, mix the ground meat, eggs, flaxseed meal, shallot, garlic, and spices thoroughly.
2. In another bowl, mix the tomato puree with the mustard and liquid monk fruit, whisk to combine well.
3. Press the mixture into the loaf pan—Bake in the preheated oven at 360°F for 30 minutes.

Nutrition for Total Servings:

- **Carbs:** 15.64 g
- **Calories:** 517
- **Fat:** 32.3g
- **Protein:** 48.5g

Rich Winter Beef Stew

Preparation time: 45 minutes
Cooking time: 50 minutes
Servings: 2
Ingredients:

- 1-ounce bacon, diced
- 3/4-pound well-marbled beef chuck, boneless and cut into 1- 1/2-inch pieces
- 1 red bell pepper, chopped
- 1 green bell pepper, chopped
- 2 garlic cloves, minced
- 1/2 cup leeks, chopped
- 1 parsnip, chopped
- Sea salt, to taste
- 1/4 tsp. mixed peppercorns, freshly cracked
- 2 cups of chicken bone broth
- 1 tomato, pureed
- 2 cups kale, torn into pieces
- 1 tbsp. fresh cilantro, roughly chopped

Kitchen Equipment:

- Dutch pot

Directions:

1. Heat a Dutch pot over medium-high flame. Now, cook the bacon until it is well browned and crisp; reserve. Then, cook the beef pieces for 3 to 5 minutes or until just browned on all sides; reserve. After that, sauté the peppers, garlic, leeks, and parsnip in the pan drippings until they are just tender and aromatic. Add the salt, peppercorns, chicken bone broth, tomato, and reserved beef to the pot. Bring to a boil. Stir in the kale leaves and continue simmering until the leaves have wilted or 3 to 4 minutes more.

2. Ladle into individual bowls & serve garnished with fresh cilantro and the reserved bacon.

Nutrition for Total Servings:

- **Carbs:** 16.14 g
- **Protein:** 88.75 g
- **Calories:** 359
- **Fat:** 17.8g

Crunchy Chicken Milanese

Preparation time: 10 minutes
Cooking time: 10 minutes
Servings: 2
Ingredients:

- 2 boneless skinless chicken breasts
- 1/2 cup coconut flour
- 1 tsp. ground cayenne pepper
- Pink Himalayan salt
- Freshly ground black pepper
- 1 egg, lightly beaten
- 1/2 cup crushed pork rinds
- 2 tbsps. olive oil

Directions:

1. Pound the chicken breasts with a heavy mallet until they are about 1/2 inch thick. (If you don't have a kitchen mallet, you can use the thick rim of a heavy plate.)
2. Prepare two separate prep plates and one small, shallow bowl
3. On plate 1, put the coconut flour, cayenne pepper, pink Himalayan salt, and pepper. Mix together.
4. Crack the egg into the small bowl, and lightly beat it with a fork or whisk.
5. On plate 2, put the crushed pork rinds.
6. In a large skillet over medium-high heat, heat the olive oil.
7. Dredge 1 chicken breast on both sides in the coconut-flour mixture. Dip the chicken into the egg, & coat both sides. Dredge the chicken in a pork-rind mixture, pressing the pork rinds into the chicken so they stick. Place the coated chicken in a hot skillet & repeat with the other chicken breast.
8. Cook the chicken for 3 to 5 minutes on each side, until brown, crispy, and cooked through, and serve.

Nutrition for Total Servings:

- **Calories:** 604
- **Fat:** 29g
- **Carbs:** 17g
- **Protein:** 65g

Spinach

Preparation time: 5 minutes
Cooking time: 25 minutes
Servings: 8
Ingredients:

- 2 (10-ounce) packages of frozen spinach, thawed & drained
- 1 1/2 cups water, divided
- 1/4 cup sour cream
- Oat milk
- 2 tbsps. butter
- 1 tbsp. onion, minced
- 1 tbsp. garlic, minced
- 1 tbsp. fresh ginger, minced
- 2 tbsps. tomato puree
- 2 teaspoons curry powder
- 2 teaspoons garam masala powder
- 2 teaspoons ground coriander
- 2 teaspoons ground cumin
- 2 teaspoons ground turmeric
- 2 teaspoons red pepper flakes, crushed
- Salt, to taste

Directions:

9. Place spinach, 1/2 cup of water, and sour cream in a blender and pulse until pureed.
10. Transfer the spinach puree into a bowl and set aside.
11. In a large non-stick wok, melt butter over medium-low heat and sauté onion, garlic, ginger, tomato puree, spices, and salt for about 2–3 minutes.
12. Add the spinach puree and remaining water and stir to combine.
13. Adjust the heat to medium & cook for about 3–5 minutes.
14. Add oat milk and stir to combine.
15. Adjust heat to low & cook for about 10–15 minutes.

16. Serve hot.

Nutrition for Total Servings:
- **Calories:** 121 Cal
- **Fat:** 12 g
- **Carbs:** 9 g
- **Protein:** 4 g

CHAPTER 6:

Poultry

Braised Chicken in Italian Tomato Sauce

Preparation time: 15 minutes
Cooking time: 4 hrs.
Servings: 4
Ingredients:
- 1/4 cup olive oil, divided
- 4 (4-ounce/113-g) boneless chicken thighs
- Pepper and salt
- 1/2 cup chicken stock
- 4 ounces (113 g) julienned oil-packed sun-dried tomatoes
- 1 (28-ounce/794-g) can sodium-free diced tomatoes
- 2 tbsps. dried oregano
- 2 tbsps. minced garlic
- Red pepper flakes, to taste
- 2 tbsps. chopped fresh parsley

Directions:
1. Heat oil then put the chicken thighs in the skillet and sprinkle salt and black pepper to season.
2. Sear the chicken thighs for 10 minutes or until well browned.
3. Flip them halfway through the cooking time.

4. Put the chicken thighs, stock, tomatoes, oregano, garlic, and red pepper flakes into the slow cooker. Stir to coat the chicken thighs well.
5. High cook for 4 hrs.
6. Transfer the chicken thighs to four plates.
7. Pour the sauce which remains in the slow cooker over the chicken thighs and top with fresh parsley before serving warm.

Nutrition for Total Servings:
- **Calories:** 464
- **Fat:** 12.1g
- **Carbs:** 6.4 g
- **Protein:** 13.1g

Cheesy Roasted Chicken

Preparation time: 15 minutes
Cooking time: 10 minutes
Servings: 6
Ingredients:
- 3 cups of chopped roasted chicken

Directions:
1. Oven: 350F
2. Be sure to rub butter or spray with non-stick cooking spray. Put in the chicken and toss thoroughly.
3. Be sure to leave space between piles.
4. Bake for 4-6 minutes. The moment they turn golden brown at the edges, take them off.
5. Serve hot.

Nutrition for Total Servings:
- **Calories**: 387
- **Fat:** 19.5g
- **Carbs:** 3.9 g
- **Protein:** 14.5g

Chicken Spinach Salad

Preparation time: 15 minutes
Cooking time: 0 minutes
Servings: 3
Ingredients:
- 2 1/2 cups of spinach
- 4 1/2 ounces of boiled chicken
- 2 boiled eggs
- 1/2 cup of chopped cucumber
- 3 slices of bacon
- 1 small avocado
- 1 tbsp. olive oil
- 1/2 tsp. of coconut oil
- Pinch of Salt
- Pepper

Directions:
1. Dice the boiled eggs.
2. Slice boiled chicken, bacon, avocado, spinach, cucumber, and combine them in a bowl. Then add diced boiled eggs.
3. Drizzle with some oil. Mix well.
4. Add salt and pepper to taste.
5. Enjoy.

Nutrition for Total Servings:
- **Calories**: 265
- **Fat:** 9.5g
- **Carbs**: 3.3 g
- **Protein:** 14.1 g

Turkey Breast with Tomato-Olive Salsa

Preparation time: 20 minutes
Cooking time: 10 minutes
Servings: 4
Ingredients:
For turkey:
- 4 boneless turkey, skinned.
- 3 tbsps. olive oil
- Salt
- Pepper

For salsa:
- 6 chopped tomatoes
- 5 ounces of pitted and chopped olives
- 2 crushed garlic cloves
- Pepper
- Salt

Directions:
1. In a bowl, put salt, pepper, and three spoons of oil, mix and coat the turkey with this mixture.
2. Place it on a preheated grill and grill for ten minutes.
3. In another bowl, mix garlic, olives, tomatoes, pepper, and drop the rest of the oil. Sprinkle salt and toss. Serve this salsa with turkey is warm.

Nutrition for Total Servings:
- **Calories:** 387
- **Fat:** 12.5g
- **Carbs:** 3.1 g
- **Protein:** 18.6g

Turkey Meatballs

Preparation time: 15 minutes
Cooking time: 20 minutes
Servings: 2
Ingredients:

- 1 pound of ground turkey
- 1 tbsp. of fish sauce
- 1 diced onion
- 2 tbsps. of soy sauce
- 1/2 almond flour
- 1/8 cup of ground beef
- 1/2 tsp. of garlic powder
- 1/2 tsp. of salt
- 1/2 tsp. of ground ginger
- 1/2 tsp. of thyme
- 1/2 tsp. of curry
- 5 tbsps. of olive oil

Directions:

1. Combine ground turkey, fish sauce, one diced onion, soy sauce, ground beef, seasonings, oil, and flour in a large mixing bowl. Mix it thoroughly.
2. Form meatballs depending on preferred size.
3. Heat skillet and pour in 3 tbsps. Of oil [you may need more depending on the size of meat balls].
4. Cook meatballs until evenly browned on each side. Serve hot.

Nutrition for Total Servings:

- **Calories:** 281
- **Fat:** 11.6g
- **Carbs**: 4.6 g
- **Protein:** 15.1g

Cheesy Bacon Ranch Chicken

Preparation time: 40 minutes
Cooking time: 35 minutes
Servings: 8
Ingredients:

- 8 boneless and skinned chicken breasts
- 1 cup of olive oil
- 8 thick slices of bacon
- 3 cups of shredded mozzarella
- 1 1/4 tbsp. of ranch seasoning
- Chopped chives
- Kosher salt or pink salt
- Black pepper

Directions:

1. Preheat skillet and heat little oil, and cook bacon evenly on both sides.
2. Save four tbsps. Of drippings and put the others away.
3. Add in salt and pepper in a bowl and rub it over chicken to season.
4. Put 1/2 oil on the flame to cook the chicken from each side for 5 to 7 minutes.
5. When ready, reduce the heat and put in the ranch seasoning, then add mozzarella.
6. Cover and cook on a low flame for 3-5 minutes.
7. Put in bacon fat and chopped chives, then bacon and cover it.
8. Take off and serve warm.

Nutrition for Total Servings:

- **Calories:** 387
- **Fat:** 15.1g
- **Carbs:** 5.9 g
- **Protein:** 12.9g

Indian Buttered Chicken

Preparation time: 15 minutes
Cooking time: 30 minutes
Servings: 4
Ingredients:

- 3 tbsps. unsalted butter
- 1 medium yellow onion, chopped
- 2 garlic cloves, minced
- 1 tsp. fresh ginger, minced
- 1 1/2 pounds grass-fed chicken breasts, cut into 3/4-inch chunks
- 2 tomatoes, chopped finely
- 1 tbsp. garam masala
- 1 tsp. red chili powder
- 1 tsp. ground cumin
- Salt and ground black pepper, as required
- 1 cup heavy cream
- 2 tbsps. fresh cilantro, chopped

Directions:

1. In a wok, melt butter and sauté the onions for about 5–6 minutes.
2. Now, add in ginger and garlic and sauté for about 1 minute.
3. Add the tomatoes and cook for about 2–3 minutes, crushing with the back of the spoon.
4. Stir in the chicken, spices, salt, and black pepper, and cook for about 6–8 minutes or until the desired doneness of the chicken.
5. Put in the cream and cook for about 8–10 more minutes, stirring occasionally.
6. Garnish with fresh cilantro and serve hot.

Nutrition for Total Servings:

- **Calories:** 456
- **Fat:** 14.1g
- **Carbs**: 6.8 g
- **Protein**: 12.8 g

Broccoli and Chicken Casserole

Preparation time: 15 minutes
Cooking time: 35 minutes
Servings: 6
Ingredients:

- 2 tbsps. butter
- 1/4 cup cooked bacon, crumbled
- 1/4 cup heavy whipping cream
- 1/2 pack ranch seasoning mix
- 2/3 cup homemade chicken broth
- 1 1/2 cups small broccoli florets
- 2 cups cooked grass-fed chicken breast, shredded

Directions:

1. Now, preheat the oven to 350°F.
2. Arrange a rack in the upper portion of the oven.
3. For the chicken mixture: In a large wok, melt the butter over low heat.
4. Add the bacon, heavy whipping cream, ranch seasoning, and broth, and with a wire whisk, beat until well combined.
5. Cook for about 5 minutes, stirring frequently.
6. Meanwhile, in a microwave-safe dish, place the broccoli and microwave until desired tenderness is achieved.
7. In the wok, add the chicken and broccoli and mix until well combined.
8. Remove from the heat and transfer the mixture into a casserole dish.
9. Top the chicken mixture
10. Bake for about 25 minutes.
11. Now, set the oven to broiler.
12. Broil the chicken mixture for about 2–3 minutes
13. Serve hot.

Nutrition for Total Servings:

- **Calories:** 431
- **Fat:** 10.5g
- **Carbs:** 4.9 g
- **Protein:** 14.1g

Chicken Parmigiana

Preparation time: 15 minutes
Cooking time: 25 minutes
Servings: 5
Ingredients:

- 5 (6-ounce) grass-fed skinless, boneless chicken breasts
- 1 large organic egg, beaten
- 1/2 cup superfine blanched almond flour
- 1/2 tsp. dried parsley
- 1/2 tsp. paprika
- 1/2 tsp. garlic powder
- Salt and ground black pepper, as required
- 1/4 cup olive oil
- 1 cup sugar-free tomato sauce
- 2 tbsps. fresh parsley, chopped
- 1/3 cup parmesan cheese

Directions:

1. Now, preheat the oven to 375°F.
2. Arrange one chicken breast between 2 pieces of parchment paper.
3. With a meat mallet, pound the chicken breast into a 1/2-inch thickness
4. Repeat with the remaining chicken breasts.
5. Add the beaten egg into a shallow dish.
6. Place the almond flour, parmesan, parsley, spices, salt, and black pepper in another shallow dish, and mix well.
7. Dip chicken breasts into the whipped egg and then coat with the flour mixture.
8. Now, preheat the oven oil in a deep wok over medium-high heat and fry the chicken breasts for about 3 minutes per side.
9. The chicken breasts must be transferred onto a paper towel-lined plate to drain.

10. At the bottom of a casserole, place about 1/2 cup of tomato sauce and spread evenly.
11. Arrange the chicken breasts over marinara sauce in a single layer.
12. Put sauce on top
13. Bake for about 20 minutes or until done completely.
14. Remove from the oven and serve hot with the garnishing of parsley.

Nutrition for Total Servings:
- **Calories:** 398
- **Fat:** 15.1g
- **Carbs:** 4.1g
- **Protein:** 15.1g

Chicken Schnitzel

Preparation time: 15 minutes
Cooking time: 15-20 minutes
Servings: 4
Ingredients:

- 1 tbsp. chopped fresh parsley
- 4 garlic cloves, minced
- 1 tbsp. plain vinegar
- 1 tbsp. coconut aminos
- 2 tsp. sugar-free maple syrup
- 2 tsp. chili pepper
- Salt and black pepper to taste
- 6 tbsp. coconut oil
- 1 lb. asparagus, hard stems removed
- 4 chicken breasts, skin-on and boneless
- 1 tbsp. mixed sesame seeds
- 1 cup almond flour
- 4 eggs, beaten
- 6 tbsp. avocado oil
- 1 tsp. chili flakes for garnish

Directions:

1. In a bowl, whisk the parsley, garlic, vinegar, coconut aminos, maple syrup, chili pepper, salt, and black pepper. Set aside.
2. Now, preheat the oven coconut oil in a large skillet and stir-fry the asparagus for 8 to 10 minutes or until tender. Remove the asparagus into a large bowl and toss with the vinegar mixture. Set aside for serving.
3. Cover the chicken breasts in plastic wraps and use a meat tenderizer to pound the chicken until flattened to 2-inch thickness gently.
4. On a plate, mix the sesame seeds. Dredge the chicken pieces in the almond flour, dip in the egg on both sides, and generously coat in the seed mix.
5. Now, preheat the oven avocado oil. Cook the chicken until golden brown and cooked within.

6. Divide the asparagus onto four serving plates, place a chicken on each, and garnish with the chili flakes. Serve warm.

Nutrition for Total Servings:

- **Calories:** 451
- **Fat:** 18.5g
- **Carbs:** 5.9 g
- **Protein:** 19.5g

Chicken Cauliflower Fried Rice

Preparation time: 15 minutes
Cooking time: 20 minutes
Servings: 4
Ingredients:

- 1/2 tsp. of sesame oil
- 1 small carrot (chopped)
- 1 tbsp. of avocado or coconut oil
- 1 small onion (finely sliced)
- 1/2 cup of snap peas (chopped)
- 1/2 cup of red peppers cut finely
- 1 tbsp. of garlic
- 1 tbsp. of garlic, properly chopped
- 1 tsp. of salt
- 2 teaspoons of garlic powder
- 4 chicken breasts, chopped and cooked
- 4 cups of rice cauliflower
- 2 large scrambled eggs
- Gluten-free soy sauce, one quarter cup size

Directions:

1. Gently season the chicken breasts with 1/2 tbsp. of salt, 1/4 tbsp. of pepper, and 1/2 tbsp. of oil. Cook the chicken on any pan of your choice
2. Add coconut/olive/avocado oil. Cut some onions and carrots and sauce and leave for up to 3 minutes
3. Next, add the rest of the vegetables, pepper/salt/garlic powder and then cook for extra 3 minutes
4. Put in fresh garlic, soy sauce and riced cauliflower; then stir
5. Add scrambled eggs and chicken and mix until they are well combined
6. Put off the heat and then stir in some green peas. Season again. You can top it with sesame seeds if you like

Nutrition for Total Servings:

- **Calories:** 271
- **Fat:** 15.1g
- **Carbs:** 3.9 g
- **Protein:** 5.1g

Greek Stuffed Chicken Breast

Preparation time: 30 minutes
Cooking time: 30 minutes
Servings: 4
Ingredients:

- 1 tbsp. butter
- 1/4 cup chopped sweet onion
- 1/4 cup Kalamata olives, chopped
- 1/4 cup chopped roasted red pepper
- 2 tbsps. chopped fresh basil
- 4 (5-ounce) chicken breasts, skin-on
- 2 tbsps. extra-virgin olive oil

Directions:

1. Now, preheat the oven to 400°F.
2. Melt some butter and add the onion. Sauté until tender, about 3 minutes.
3. The onion must be added to a bowl then continue putting olives, red pepper, and basil. Stir until well blended, then refrigerate for about 30 minutes.
4. Cut horizontal pockets into each chicken breast, and stuff them evenly with the filling. Secure the two sides of each breast with toothpicks.
5. Heat oil in a preheated pan. The chicken must be browned per side.
6. Roast in the oven for 15 minutes. Remove the toothpicks and serve.

Nutrition for Total Servings:

- **Calories:** 381
- **Fat:** 15.9g
- **Carbs:** 3.9 g
- **Protein:** 14.1g

Chicken Meatloaf Cups with Pancetta

Preparation time: 15 minutes
Cooking time: 30 minutes
Servings: 6
Ingredients:

- 2 tbsp. onion, chopped
- 1 tsp. garlic, minced
- 1-pound ground chicken
- 2 ounces cooked pancetta, chopped
- 1 egg, beaten
- 1 tsp. mustard
- Salt and black pepper, to taste
- 1/2 tsp. crushed red pepper flakes
- 1 tsp. dried basil
- 1/2 tsp. dried oregano

Directions:

1. In a mixing bowl, mix mustard, onion, ground chicken, egg, bacon, pancetta and garlic. Season with oregano, red pepper, black pepper, basil, and salt.
2. Split the mixture into muffin cups Close the top
3. Bake in the oven at 345°F for 20 minutes, or until the meatloaf cups become golden brown.

Nutrition for Total Servings:

- **Calories:** 231
- **Fat:** 10.4g
- **Carbs:** 3.9 g
- **Protein:** 11.4g

Thai Peanut Chicken Skewers

Preparation time: 10 minutes
Cooking time: 15 minutes
Servings: 2
Ingredients:

- 1-pound boneless skinless chicken breast, cut into chunks
- 3 tbsps. Soy sauce
- 1/2 tsp. Sriracha sauce, plus 1/4 tsp.
- 3 teaspoons toasted sesame oil, divided
- Ghee, for oiling
- 2 tbsps. peanut butter
- Pink Himalayan salt
- Freshly ground black pepper

Directions:

1. In a bag, combine the chicken chunks with two tbsps. Of soy sauce, 1/2 tsp. of Sriracha sauce, and two teaspoons of sesame oil. Marinate the chicken.
2. If you are using wood 8-inch skewers, soak them in water for 30 minutes before using them.
3. Oil the grill pan with ghee.
4. Thread chicken chunks into skewers.
5. Cook skewers over low heat 10 to 15 min, flipping halfway through.
6. Next, mix the peanut dipping sauce.
7. Stir remaining one tbsp. of soy sauce, 1/4 tsp. of Sriracha sauce, one tsp. of sesame oil, and peanut butter.
8. Season with pink Himalayan salt and pepper.
9. Serve the chicken skewers with a small dish of peanut sauce.

Nutrition for Total Servings:

- **Calories**: 390
- **Fat**: 18.4 g
- **Carbs**: 2.1 g
- **Protein**: 17.4g

Tuscan Chicken

Preparation time: 15 minutes
Cooking time: 15 minutes
Servings: 6
Ingredients:
- 1 1/2 pounds chicken breasts, pasteurized, skinless, thinly sliced
- 1/2 cup sun-dried tomatoes
- 1 cup spinach, chopped
- 1 tsp. garlic powder
- 1 tsp. Italian seasoning
- 2 tbsps. avocado oil
- 1 cup heavy cream, full-fat

Directions:
1. Take a large skillet pan, place it over medium-high heat, add oil, and when hot, add chicken and then cook for 3–5 minutes per side until golden brown.
2. Add garlic powder, Italian seasoning, and pour in the cream, and then whisk until combined.
3. Switch heat to medium-high, cook the sauce for 2 minutes until it begins to thicken, then add tomatoes and spinach and simmer until spinach leaves begin to wilt.
4. Return chicken to the pan, toss until mixed and cook for 2 minutes until hot.
5. Serve chicken with cooked keto pasta, such as zucchini noodles.

Nutrition for Total Servings:
- **Calories:** 390
- **Fat:** 16.1g
- **Carbs:** 3g
- **Protein:** 19g

Chicken Pot Pie

Preparation time: 15 minutes
Cooking time: 25 minutes
Servings: 4
Ingredients:
For the filling:
- 1/2 medium onion, chopped
- 2 celery stalks, chopped
- 1/2 cup fresh or frozen peas
- 2 tbsps. butter
- 1 garlic clove, minced
- 1 1/2 pounds chicken thighs
- 1 cup chicken broth
- 1/2 cup heavy (whipping) cream
- 1 tsp. dried thyme
- 1/2 tsp. pink Himalayan sea salt
- 1/2 tsp. freshly ground black pepper

For the crust:
- 1 cup almond flour
- 2 tbsps. butter, at room temperature
- 2 tbsps. sour cream
- 1 large egg white
- 1 tbsp. ground flaxseed
- 1 tsp. xanthan gum
- 1 tsp. baking powder
- 1/2 tsp. garlic powder
- 1/4 tsp. pink Himalayan sea salt
- 1/4 tsp. dried thyme

Directions:
1. Filling: In a saucepan, combine the onion, celery, peas, butter, and garlic over medium heat.

2. Cook for about 5 minutes, until the onion starts to turn translucent.
3. In a large skillet, cook the chicken thighs for 3 to 5 minutes, until there is no more visible pink. Add the cooked chicken and all juices to the pan with the vegetables.
4. Add the broth, cream, thyme, salt, and pepper to the pan. Simmer it until sauce thickens, stirring occasionally.
5. Now, preheat the oven to 400°F.
6. In a bowl or container, combine the almond flour, butter, sour cream, egg white, flaxseed, xanthan gum, baking powder, garlic powder, salt, and thyme.
7. Form this into a dough.
8. Place the dough between 2 sheets of parchment paper and roll out into a 10-inch round that is 1/4 inch thick.
9. Fill an 8-inch pie pan or 4 (6-ounce) ramekins with the chicken filling.
10. Top the pie pan with the crust, flipping it onto the filling and peeling away the parchment paper. If using ramekins, cut circles of the dough and fit them onto the ramekins.
11. Pinch to seal the edges, and trim off any excess.
12. Baking time: 10-12 minutes
13. Let cool for 5 minutes, then serve.

Nutrition for Total Servings:
- **Calories:** 341
- **Fat:** 18.4g
- **Carb:** 4.1 g
- **Protein:** 12.5g

Thai Chicken Salad Bowl

Preparation time: 12 minutes
Cooking time: 15 minutes
Servings: 2
Ingredients:
Marinade:

- 1 clove garlic, minced
- 1 tbsp. grated ginger
- 1 small red chili, finely chopped
- 1/2 stalk lemongrass, finely chopped
- 2 tbsp. fresh lime juice
- 1 tsp. fish sauce
- 1 tbsp. coconut aminos

Salad:

- 8 oz. (226g) (2-pieces) chicken breasts
- 1/2 cup shredded red cabbage
- 1/2 cup shredded green cabbage
- 2/3 cup grated carrot
- 1 tbsp. chopped mint
- 1/2 cup chopped cilantro
- 1 tbsp. chopped chives
- 1/4 cup blanched almonds

Dressing:

- 3 tbsp. extra virgin olive oil
- Salt and pepper, to taste

Directions:

1. Oven: 400 F
2. Combine the garlic, ginger, red chili, lemongrass, lime juice, fish sauce, and coconut aminos in a bowl for marinating and crush with a mortar.
3. Flatten the chicken breasts with a meat mallet.
4. Add the chicken to a bowl and add half of the marinade, and coat the chicken evenly.
5. Make it cool in the refrigerator for a maximum of 30 minutes or an hour.
6. Combine both cabbages, carrot, mint, cilantro, and chives in a bowl.
7. In a baking tray, spread out the almonds and roast in the oven for 5-8 minutes, set aside.
8. Grill the chicken in a griddle.
9. Cook through then slice.
10. Mix in the remaining ingredients.

Nutrition for Total Servings:

- **Calories**: 351
- **Fat:** 15.7g
- **Carbs:** 3.1 g
- **Protein:** 12.5g

Chicken Rollatini

Preparation time: 15 minutes
Cooking time: 30 minutes
Servings: 4
Ingredients:

- 4 (3-ounce) boneless skinless chicken breasts, pounded to about 1/3 inch thick
- 4 slices prosciutto (4 ounces)
- 1 cup fresh spinach
- 1/2 cup almond flour
- 2 eggs, beaten
- 1/4 cup good-quality olive oil
- 1/3 cup parmesan cheese
- 8 ounces ricotta cheese

Directions:

1. Now, preheat the oven. Set the oven temperature to 400°F.
2. Prepare the chicken—Pat the chicken breasts dry with paper towels. Spread 1/4 of the ricotta in the middle of each breast.
3. Place the prosciutto over the ricotta and 1/4 cup of the spinach on the prosciutto.
4. Fold the long edges of the chicken breast over the filling, then roll the chicken breast up to enclose the filling.
5. Place the rolls seam-side down on your work surface.
6. Bread the chicken. On a plate, stir together the almond flour and parmesan and set it next to the beaten eggs.
7. Carefully dip a chicken roll in the egg, then roll it in the almond-flour mixture until it is completely covered.
8. Set the rolls seam-side down on your work surface. Repeat with the other rolls.
9. Brown the rolls. In a medium skillet over medium heat, warm the olive oil.
10. Place the rolls seam-side down in the skillet and brown them on all sides, turning them carefully, about 10 minutes in total.
11. Transfer the rolls, seam-side down, to a 9-by-9-inch baking dish—Bake the chicken rolls for 25 minutes, or until they're cooked through.
12. Serve. Place one chicken roll on each of four plates and serve them immediately.

Nutrition for Total Servings:

- **Calories:** 365
- **Fat:** 17.1g
- **Carbs:** 3.2 g
- **Protein:** 1.4g

Gravy Bacon and Turkey

Preparation time: 15 minutes
Cooking time: 3 hours
Servings: 14
Ingredients:
- 12 pounds (5.4 kg) turkey
- Sea salt and fresh ground black pepper, to taste
- 1 pound (454 g) cherry tomatoes
- 1 cup red onions, diced
- 2 garlic cloves, minced
- 1 large celery stalk, diced
- 4 teaspoons fresh thyme, four small sprigs
- 8 ounces (227 g) bacon (10 slices, diced)
- 8 tbsps. butter
- 2 lemons, the juice
- 1/8 teaspoon guar gum (optional)

Directions:
1. Start by preheating the oven to 350°F (180°C).
2. Remove the neck and giblets from the turkey, pat the turkey dry with paper towels and season both inside and outside of the turkey with salt and pepper.
3. Insert cherry tomatoes, onions, celery, garlic and thyme into the turkey cavity. Tie the legs together with kitchen twine, and put the turkey on a large roasting pan, tuck its wings under the body.
4. Cook the bacon in a large skillet over medium heat until crisp, for 7 to 8 mins. Transfer to paper towels to drain, reserving the drippings in the skillet.
5. Add the ghee or butter to the skillet with the drippings & stir until melted, then pour into a bowl and stir in the lemon juice. Rub mixture all over the turkey.
6. Place into the oven for 30 minutes. After every 30 minutes, baste the turkey with the drippings. Roast for about 3 hrs. Or until a thermometer inserted into the thigh registers 165°F (74°C).
7. Remove from oven onto a serving tray to rest for at least 25 minutes before serving.
8. Meanwhile, pour the drippings into a saucepan. Whisk in the guar gum to thicken, after 2 minutes of whisking, add a touch more if you want a thicker gravy. Then add the reserved bacon for one amazing gravy.

Nutrition for Total Servings:
- **Calories**: 693
- **Fat:** 35.0g
- **Carbs:** 3.7g
- **Protein**: 86.7g

Creamy Chicken Bake

Preparation time: 15 minutes
Cooking time: 70 minutes
Servings: 6
Ingredients:
- 5 tbsps. unsalted butter, divided
- 2 small onions, sliced thinly
- 3 garlic cloves, minced
- 1 tsp. dried tarragon, crushed
- 1 cup homemade chicken broth, divided
- 2 tbsps. fresh lemon juice
- 1/2 cup heavy cream
- 1 1/2 teaspoons Herbs de Provence
- Salt and ground black pepper, to taste
- 4 (6-ounce) grass-fed chicken breasts

Directions:
1. Now, preheat the oven to 3500F.
2. Grease a 13x9-inch baking plate with 1 tbsp. of butter.
3. In a wok, melt 2 tbsps. Of butter over medium heat and sauté the onion, garlic, and tarragon for about 4–5 minutes.
4. Transfer the onion mixture onto a plate.
5. In the same wok, melt the remaining 2 tbsps. butter over low heat, 1/2 cup of broth, and lemon juice for about 3–4 minutes stirring continuously.
6. Stir in the cream, herbs de Provence, salt, and black pepper, and remove from heat.
7. Pour remaining broth in a prepared baking dish.
8. Arrange chicken breasts in the baking dish in a single layer and top with the cream mixture evenly.
9. Bake for approximately 45–60 minutes.
10. Serve hot.

Nutrition for Total Servings:
- **Calories**: 129 Cal
- **Fat:** 12 g
- **Carbs:** 9 g
- **Protein:** 7 g

Chicken-Basil Alfredo with Shirataki Noodles

Preparation time: 10 minutes
Cooking time: 15 minutes
Servings: 2
Ingredients:
For the noodles:
- 1 (7-ounce) package Miracle Noodle Fettuccini, Shirataki Noodles

For the sauce:
- 1 tbsp. olive oil
- 4 ounces cooked shredded chicken (I usually use a store-bought rotisserie chicken)
- Pink Himalayan salt
- Freshly ground black pepper
- 1 cup Alfredo Sauce, or any brand you like
- 2 tbsps. chopped fresh basil leaves

Directions:
1. In a colander, rinse the noodles with cold water (shirataki noodles naturally have a smell, and rinsing with cold water will help remove this).
2. Fill a large saucepan with water & bring to a boil over high heat. Add the noodles & boil for 2 minutes. Drain.
3. Transfer the noodles to a large, dry skillet over medium-low heat to evaporate any moisture. Do not grease the skillet; it must be dry. Transfer the noodles to a plate and set them aside.

To make the sauce:
4. In the saucepan over medium heat, heat the olive oil. Add the cooked chicken. Season with pink Himalayan salt and pepper.
5. Pour the Alfredo sauce over the chicken, and cook until warm. Season with more pink Himalayan salt and pepper.
6. Add the dried noodles to the sauce mixture, and toss until combined.
7. Divide the pasta between two plates, and chopped basil, and serve.

Nutrition for Total Servings:
- **Calories:** 673
- **Fat:** 61g
- **Carbs:** 4g
- **Protein:** 29g

Chicken Quesadilla

Preparation time: 5 minutes
Cooking time: 5 minutes
Servings: 2
Ingredients:
- 1 tbsp. olive oil
- 2 low-carbohydrate tortillas
- 2 ounces shredded chicken (I usually use a store-bought rotisserie chicken)
- 1 tsp. Tajín seasoning salt
- 2 tbsps. sour cream

Directions:
1. In a large skillet over medium-high heat, heat the olive oil. Add a tortilla, the chicken, the Tajín seasoning. Top with the second tortilla.
2. Peek under the edge of the bottom tortilla to monitor how it is browning. Once the bottom tortilla gets golden flip the quesadilla over. The second side will cook faster, about 1 minute.
3. Once the second tortilla is crispy and golden, transfer the quesadilla to a cutting board and let sit for 2 minutes. Cut the quesadilla into 4 wedges using a pizza cutter or chef's knife.
4. Transfer half the quesadilla to each of two plates. Add 1 tbsp. of sour cream to each plate, and serve hot.

Nutrition for Total Servings:
- **Calories:** 414
- **Fat:** 28g
- **Carbs**: 24g
- **Protein:** 26g

Braised Chicken Thighs with Kalamata Olives

Preparation time: 10 minutes
Cooking time: 40 minutes
Servings: 2
Ingredients:
- 4 chicken thighs, skin on
- Pink Himalayan salt
- Freshly ground black pepper
- 2 tbsps. ghee
- 1/2 cup chicken broth
- 1 lemon, 1/2 sliced and 1/2 juiced
- 1/2 cup pitted Kalamata olives
- 2 tbsps. butter

Directions:
1. Now, preheat the oven to 375°F.
2. Pat the chicken thighs dry with paper towels, and season with pink Himalayan salt and pepper.
3. In a medium oven-safe skillet or high-sided baking dish over medium-high heat, melt the ghee. When the ghee has melted and is hot, add the chicken thighs, skin-side down, and leave them for about 8 minutes, or until the skin is brown and crispy.
4. Flip the chicken and cook for 2 minutes on the second side. Around the chicken thighs, pour in the chicken broth, and add the lemon slices, lemon juice, and olives.
5. Bake in the oven for about 30 minutes, until the chicken is cooked through.
6. Add the butter to the broth mixture.
7. Divide the chicken and olives between two plates and serve.

Nutrition for Total Servings:
- **Calories:** 567
- **Fat:** 47g
- **Carbs:** 4g
- **Protein:** 33g

Buttery Garlic Chicken

Preparation time: 5 minutes
Cooking time: 40 minutes
Servings: 2
Ingredients:

- 2 tbsps. ghee, melted
- Boneless skinless chicken breasts
- Pink Himalayan salt
- Freshly ground black pepper
- 1 tbsp. dried Italian seasoning
- 4 tbsps. butter
- 2 garlic cloves, minced

Directions:

1. Now, preheat the oven to 375°F. Choose a baking dish that is large enough to hold both chicken breasts and coat it with ghee.
2. Pat dry the chicken breasts and season with pink Himalayan salt, pepper, and Italian seasoning. Place the chicken in the baking dish.
3. In a medium skillet over medium heat, melt the butter. Add the minced garlic, and cook for about 5 minutes. You want the garlic very lightly browned but not burned.
4. Remove the butter-garlic mixture from the heat, and pour it over the chicken breasts.
5. Roast the chicken in the oven for 30 to 35 minutes, until cooked through. . Let the chicken rest in the baking dish for 5 minutes.
6. Divide the chicken between two plates, spoon the butter sauce over the chicken, and serve.

Nutrition for Total Servings:

- **Calories**: 642
- **Fat:** 45g
- **Carbs**: 2g
- **Protein:** 57g

Parmesan Baked Chicken

Preparation time: 5 minutes
Cooking time: 20 minutes
Servings: 2
Ingredients:

- 2 tbsps. ghee
- 2 boneless skinless chicken breasts
- Pink Himalayan salt
- Freshly ground black pepper
- 1/2 cup mayonnaise
- 1 tbsp. dried Italian seasoning
- 1/4 cup crushed pork rinds

Directions:

1. Now, preheat the oven to 425°F. Choose a baking dish that is large enough to hold both chicken breasts and coat it with ghee.
2. Pat dry the chicken breasts with a paper towel, season with pink Himalayan salt and pepper, and place in the prepared baking dish.
3. In a small bowl, mix to combine the mayonnaise, and Italian seasoning.
4. Slather the mayonnaise mixture evenly over the chicken breasts, and sprinkle the crushed pork rinds on top of the mayonnaise mixture.
5. Bake until the topping is browned, about 20 minutes, and serve.

Nutrition for Total Servings:

- **Calories:** 850
- **Fat:** 67g
- **Carbs:** 2g
- **Protein:** 60g

Crunchy Chicken Milanese

Preparation time: 10 minutes
Cooking time: 10 minutes
Servings: 2
Ingredients:
- 2 boneless skinless chicken breasts
- 1/2 cup coconut flour
- 1 tsp. ground cayenne pepper
- Pink Himalayan salt
- Freshly ground black pepper
- 1 egg, lightly beaten
- 1/2 cup crushed pork rinds
- 2 tbsps. olive oil

Directions:
9. Pound the chicken breasts with a heavy mallet until they are about 1/2 inch thick. (If you don't have a kitchen mallet, you can use the thick rim of a heavy plate.)
10. Prepare two separate prep plates and one small, shallow bowl
11. On plate 1, put the coconut flour, cayenne pepper, pink Himalayan salt, and pepper. Mix together.
12. Crack the egg into the small bowl, and lightly beat it with a fork or whisk.
13. On plate 2, put the crushed pork rinds.
14. In a large skillet over medium-high heat, heat the olive oil.
15. Dredge 1 chicken breast on both sides in the coconut-flour mixture. Dip the chicken into the egg, & coat both sides. Dredge the chicken in a pork-rind mixture, pressing the pork rinds into the chicken so they stick. Place the coated chicken in a hot skillet & repeat with the other chicken breast.
16. Cook the chicken for 3 to 5 minutes on each side, until brown, crispy, and cooked through, and serve.

Nutrition for Total Servings:
- **Calories:** 604
- **Fat:** 29g
- **Carbs:** 17g
- **Protein:** 65g

Egg Butter

Preparation time: 5 minutes
Cooking time: 0 minutes
Servings: 2
Ingredients:
- 2 large eggs, hard-boiled
- 3-ounce unsalted butter
- 1/2 tsp. dried oregano
- 1/2 tsp. dried basil
- 2 leaves of iceberg lettuce

Seasoning:
- 1/2 tsp. of sea salt
- 1/4 tsp. ground black pepper

Directions:
1. Peel the eggs, then chop them finely and place in a medium bowl.
2. Add remaining ingredients and stir well.
3. Serve egg butter wrapped in a lettuce leaf.

Nutrition for Total Servings:
- **Calories:** 159
- **Fats:** 16.5 g
- **Protein**: 3 g
- **Carbs**: 0.2 g

Cider Chicken

Preparation time: 10 minutes
Cooking time: 18 minutes
Servings: 2
Ingredients:
- 2 chicken thighs
- 1/4 cup apple cider vinegar
- 1 tsp. liquid stevia

Seasoning:
- 1/2 tbsp. coconut oil
- 1/3 tsp. salt
- 1/4 tsp. ground black pepper

Directions:
1. Turn on the oven, then set it to 450°F and let it preheat.
2. Meanwhile, place chicken in a bowl, drizzle with oil and then season with salt and black pepper
3. Take a baking sheet, place prepared chicken thighs on it, and bake for 10 to 15 minutes or until its internal temperature reaches 165°F.
4. In the meantime, take a small saucepan, place it over medium heat, pour in vinegar, stir in stevia and bring the mixture to boil.
5. Then switch heat to the low level and simmer sauce for 3 to 5 minutes until reduced by half, set aside until required.
6. When the chicken has roasted, brush it generously with prepared cider sauce, then Turn on the broiler and bake the chicken for 3 minutes until golden brown.
7. Serve.

Nutrition for Total Servings:
- **Calories:** 182.5
- **Fat:** 107.5 g
- **Protein:** 15.5 g
- **Carb:** 2.5 g

Bacon-Wrapped Chicken Bites

Preparation time: 10 minutes
Cooking time: 20 minutes
Servings: 2
Ingredients:
- 1 chicken thigh, debone, cut into small pieces
- 4 slices of bacon, cut into thirds
- 2 tbsp. garlic powder

Seasoning:
- 1/4 tsp. salt
- 1/8 tsp. ground black pepper

Directions:
1. Turn on the oven, then set it to 400°F and let it preheat.
2. Cut chicken into small pieces, then place them in a bowl, add salt, garlic powder, and black pepper and toss until well coated.
3. Wrap each chicken piece with a bacon strip, place in a baking dish and bake for 15 to 20 minutes until crispy, turning carefully every 5 minutes.
4. Serve.

Nutrition for Total Servings:
- **Calories:** 153
- **Fat:** 8.7 g
- **Protein:** 15 g
- **Carbs:** 2.7 g

Beans and Sausage

Preparation time: 5 minutes
Cooking time: 6 minutes
Servings: 2
Ingredients:
- 4 oz. green beans
- 4 oz. chicken sausage, sliced
- 1/2 tsp. dried basil
- 1/2 tsp. dried oregano
- 1/3 cup chicken broth, from chicken sausage

Seasoning:
- 1 tbsp. avocado oil
- 1/4 tsp. salt
- 1/8 tsp. ground black pepper

Directions:
1. Turn on the instant pot, place all the ingredients in its inner pot and shut with lid, in the sealed position.
2. Press the "manual" button, cook for 6 minutes at high-pressure settings and, when done, do a quick pressure release.
3. Serve immediately.

Nutrition for Total Servings:
- **Calories:** 151
- **Fats** 9.4 g
- **Protein:** 11.7 g
- **Carbs:** 3.4 g

Paprika Rubbed Chicken

Preparation time: 5 minutes
Cooking time: 25 minutes
Servings: 2
Ingredients:

- 2 chicken thighs, boneless
- 1/4 tbsp. fennel seeds, ground
- 1/2 tsp. hot paprika
- 1/4 tsp. smoked paprika
- 1/2 tsp. minced garlic

Seasoning:

- 1/4 tsp. salt
- 2 tbsp. avocado oil

Directions:

1. Turn on the oven, then set it to 325°F and let it preheat.
2. Prepare the spice mix and for this, take a small bowl, add all the ingredients in it, except for chicken, and stir until well mixed.
3. Brush the mixture on all sides of the chicken, rub it well into the meat, then place chicken onto a baking sheet and roast for 15 to 25 minutes until thoroughly cooked, basting every 10 minutes with the drippings.
4. Serve.

Nutrition for Total Servings:

- **Calories**: 102.3
- **Fat:** 8 g
- **Protein**: 7.2 g
- **Carbs:** 0.3 g

Teriyaki Chicken

Preparation time: 5 minutes
Cooking time: 18 minutes
Servings: 2
Ingredients:
- 2 chicken thighs, boneless
- 2 tbsp. soy sauce
- 1 tbsp. swerve sweetener
- 1 tbsp. avocado oil

Directions:
1. Take a skillet pan, place it over medium heat, add oil and when hot, add chicken thighs and cook for 5 minutes per side until seared.
2. Then sprinkle sugar over chicken thighs, drizzle with soy sauce and bring the sauce to boil.
3. Switch heat to medium-low level, continue cooking for 3 minutes until chicken is evenly glazed, and then transfer to a plate.
4. Serve chicken with cauliflower rice.

Nutrition for Total Servings:
- **Calories:** 150
- **Fat:** 9 g
- **Protein:** 17.3 g
- **Carbs:** 0 g

Chili Lime Chicken with Coleslaw

Preparation time: 35 minutes
Cooking time: 8 minutes
Servings: 2
Ingredients:
- 1 chicken thigh, boneless
- 2 oz. coleslaw
- 1/4 tsp. minced garlic
- 3/4 tbsp. apple cider vinegar
- 1/2 of a lime, juiced, zested

Seasoning:
- 1/4 tsp. paprika
- 1/4 tsp. salt
- 2 tbsp. avocado oil
- 1 tbsp. unsalted butter

Directions:
1. Prepare the marinade and for this, take a medium bowl, add vinegar, oil, garlic, paprika, salt, lime juice, and zest and stir until well mixed.
2. Cut chicken thighs into bite-size pieces, toss until well mixed, and marinate it in the refrigerator for 30 minutes.
3. Then take a skillet pan, place it over medium-high heat, add butter and marinated chicken pieces and cook for 8 minutes until golden brown and thoroughly cooked.
4. Serve chicken with coleslaw.

Nutrition for Total Servings:
- **Calories:** 157.3
- **Fat:** 12.8 g
- **Protein:** 9 g
- **Carbs:** 1 g

Lime Garlic Chicken Thighs

Preparation time: 35 minutes
Cooking time: 15 minutes
Servings: 2
Ingredients:
- 2 boneless chicken thighs, skinless
- 3/4 tsp. garlic powder
- 1 1/2 tsp. all-purpose seasoning
- 1/2 of lime, juiced, zested
- 1 1/2 tbsp. avocado oil

Directions:
1. Take a medium bowl, place chicken in it, and sprinkle with garlic powder, all-purpose seasoning, and lime zest.
2. Drizzle with lime juice, toss until well coated and let chicken thighs marinate for 30 minutes.
3. Then take a medium skillet pan, place it over medium heat, add oil and when hot, place marinated chicken thighs in it and cook for 5 to 7 minutes per side until thoroughly cooked.
4. Serve.

Nutrition for Total Servings:
- **Calories:** 260
- **Fat:** 15.6 g
- **Protein:** 26.8 g
- **Carbs:** 1.3 g

Chicken and Peanut Stir-Fry

Preparation time: 5 minutes
Cooking time: 5 minutes
Servings: 2
Ingredients:
- 2 chicken thighs, cubed
- 1/2 cup broccoli florets
- 1/4 cup peanuts
- 1 tbsp. sesame oil
- 1 1/2 tbsp. soy sauce

Seasoning:
- 1/2 tsp. garlic powder

Directions:
1. Take a skillet pan, place it over medium heat, add 1/2 tbsp. oil and when hot, add chicken cubes and cook for 4 minutes until browned on all sides.
2. Then add broccoli florets and continue cooking for 2 minutes until tender-crisp.
3. Add remaining ingredients, stir well and cook for another 2 minutes.
4. Serve.

Nutrition for Total Servings:
- **Calories:** 266
- **Fat:** 19 g
- **Protein:** 18.5 g
- **Carbs**: 4 g

Garlic Cheddar Chicken Thighs

Preparation time: 5 minutes
Cooking time: 25 minutes
Servings: 2
Ingredients:
- 2 chicken thighs
- 1/3 tsp. garlic powder
- 1/3 tbsp. dried basil
- 1/2 tsp. coconut oil

Seasoning:
- 1/8 tsp. salt
- 1/3 tsp. ground black pepper

Directions:
1. Turn on the oven, then set it to 450°F, and let preheat.
2. Meanwhile, prepare the herb mix and for this, stir together 1/4 tsp. oil, salt, garlic, black pepper, and basil until combined.
3. Create a pocket into each chicken thigh and then stuff it with half of the prepared herb mix and spread the remaining herb mix evenly on chicken thighs.
4. Take a skillet pan, place it over medium-high heat, add remaining oil and when hot, place stuffed chicken thighs in it and cook for 4 minutes.
5. Then flip the chicken thighs, cook for 5 to 7 minutes until the chicken is no longer pink and then roast the chicken thighs for 10 to 12 minutes until a meat thermometer inserted into the thickest part of the thighs read 160°F.
6. Let chicken thighs rest for 5 minutes and then serve.

Nutrition for Total Servings:
- **Calories**: 128.5
- **Fat:** 9.5 g
- **Protein**: 9 g
- **Carbs**: 0.2 g

Garlic Chicken Low-Carb

Preparation time: 15 Minutes
Cooking time: 45 minutes
Servings: 4
Ingredients:

- 2 ounces (57 g) butter
- 2 pounds (907 g) chicken drumsticks
- Salt & freshly ground black pepper, to taste
- 2 tbsps. olive oil
- 1 lemon, the juice
- 7 garlic cloves, sliced
- 1/2 cup fresh parsley, finely chopped

Directions:

1. Start by preheating the oven to 450°F (235°C).
2. Grease the baking pan with butter and put the chicken drumsticks, season with salt and pepper generously.
3. Drizzle the olive oil and lemon juice over the chicken pieces. Sprinkle the garlic and parsley on top.
4. Bake the chicken for 30 to 40 minutes or until the garlic slices become golden and chicken pieces turn brown and roasted, the baking time may be longer if your drumsticks are a large size. Lower the temperature considerably towards the end.

Nutrition for Total Servings:

- **Calories:** 542
- **Fat:** 40.0g
- **Carbs:** 4.0g
- **Protein:** 42.0g

Chicken and Herb Butter with Keto Zucchini Roll-Ups

Preparation time: 15 minutes
Cooking time: 40 minutes
Servings: 4
Ingredients:
Zucchini roll-ups:

- 1 1/2 pounds (680 g) zucchini
- 1/2 tsp. salt
- 3 ounces (85 g) butter
- 6 ounces (170 g) mushrooms, finely chopped
- 1/2 green bell pepper, chopped
- 2 ounces (57 g) air-dried chorizo, chopped
- 1 egg
- 1 tsp. onion powder
- 2 tbsps. fresh parsley, chopped
- 1/2 tsp. salt
- 1/4 tsp. pepper

Chicken:

- 4 (6-ounce/170-g) chicken breasts
- Salt & freshly ground pepper, to taste
- 1 ounce (28 g) butter, for frying

Herb butter:

- 4 ounces (113 g) butter, at room temperature
- 1 garlic clove
- 1/2 tsp. garlic powder
- 1 tbsp. fresh parsley, finely chopped
- 1 tsp. lemon juice
- 1/2 tsp. salt

Directions:

1. Now, preheat the oven to 350°F (180°C). Cut the zucchini lengthwise into equal slices, half an inch, Pat dry with paper towels or a clean kitchen towel and place it on a baking tray lined with parchment paper. Sprinkle salt on the zucchini and let stand for 10 minutes.
2. Bake for 20 minutes in the oven, or until the zucchini is tender. Transfer to a cooling rack from the oven, Dry more if needed.
3. Put the butter in the saucepan over medium heat, cut the mushrooms and put it in and stir fry well, let cool.
4. Add the remaining ingredients for the zucchini roll-ups to a bowl. Add the mushrooms and blend well.
5. Roll up and put it inside the baking dish with seams down Raise the temperature to 400°F (205°C). Bake for 20 minutes In the meantime, season

your chicken and fry it over medium heat in butter until it is crispy on the outside and cooked through.

Herb butter:

1. To prepare Herb butter mix the butter, garlic, garlic powder, fresh parsley, lemon juice, and salt. Thoroughly in a small bowl. Let sit for 30 minutes and serve on top of the chicken and zucchini roll-ups.

Nutrition for Total Servings:

- **Calories**: 913
- **Fat**: 84.0g
- **Carbs**: 10.0g
- **Protein**: 30.0g

Keto Buffalo Drumsticks with Chili Aioli and Garlic

Preparation time: 10 minutes
Cooking time: 40 minutes
Servings: 4
Ingredients:

- 2 pounds (907g) chicken drumsticks or chicken wings
- 1/3 cup mayonnaise, keto-friendly
- 1 tbsp. smoked paprika powder or smoked chili powder
- 1 garlic clove, minced
- 2 tbsps. olive oil, and more for greasing the baking dish
- 2 tbsps. white wine vinegar
- 1 tsp. salt
- 1 tsp. paprika powder
- 1 tbsp. tabasco

Directions:

1. Now, preheat the oven to 450°F (235°C).
2. Make the chili aioli: Combine the mayonnaise, smoked paprika powder, garlic clove, olive oil white wine vinegar, salt, paprika powder and tabasco for the marinade in a small bowl,
3. Put the drumsticks in a plastic bag, and pour the chili aioli into the plastic bag. Shake the bag thoroughly and let marinate for 10 minutes at room temperature.
4. Coat a baking dish with olive oil. Place the drumsticks in the baking dish and let bake in the preheated oven for 30 to 40 minutes or until they are done and have turned a nice color.
5. Remove the chicken wings from the oven and serve warm.

Nutrition for Total Servings:

- **Calories**: 570
- **Fat**: 43.0g
- **Carbs**: 3.0g
- **Protein**: 43.0g

Coleslaw with Crunchy Keto Chicken Thighs

Preparation time: 15 minutes
Cooking time: 40 minutes
Servings: 8
Ingredients:
- 1 tsp. salt
- 1/2 cup sour cream
- 2 tbsps. jerk seasoning (cinnamon, paprika, turmeric, ginger, saffron and cumin)
- 2 pounds (907 g) chicken thighs
- 5 ounces (142 g) pork rinds
- 3 ounces (85 g) unsweetened shredded coconut
- 3 tbsps. olive oil
- 1 pound (454 g) green cabbage
- 1 cup mayonnaise, keto-friendly
- Salt & freshly ground black pepper, to taste
- 2 big plastic bags

Directions:
1. Now, preheat the oven to 350°F (180°C).
2. Mix together a marinade of jerk seasoning, salt and sour cream. And pour in a big plastic bag with the drumsticks, please keep the skin on the drumsticks.
3. Thoroughly shake and allow to marinate for 15 minutes.
4. Take the drumsticks out, and into a new, clean bag.
5. Put the pork rinds into a food processor and blend into fine crumbs, add in coconut flakes and blend a few more seconds.
6. Pour the pork mixture into the bag with the marinated chicken and shake.
7. Grease a baking dish, and put the chicken into it, drizzle with olive oil and bake for 40 to 50 minutes, or until the chicken is cooked through. Turn the drumsticks halfway through, if the breading has already turned a desirable golden brown color, lower the heat.
8. In the meantime, cut the cabbage finely with a sharp knife or with a mandolin or even a food processor. Put the coleslaw into a bowl, season with salt and pepper, and add mayonnaise, mix well and let sit for 10 minutes.

Nutrition for Total Servings:
- **Calories:** 586
- **Fat:** 51.2g
- **Carbs:** 6.4g
- **Protein:** 27.2g

CHAPTER 7:

Beef Lamb and Pork

Jerk Pork

Preparation time: 15 minutes
Cooking time: 20 minutes
Servings: 6
Ingredients:
- 1/8 tsp cayenne pepper
- 1/4 tsp. salt
- 1/4 tsp. freshly ground black pepper
- 1/2 tbsp. dried thyme
- 1/2 tbsp. garlic powder
- 1/2 tbsp. ground allspice
- 1 tsp. ground cinnamon
- 1 tbsp. granulated erythritol
- 1 (1-pound/454-g) pork tenderloin, cut into 1-inch rounds
- 1/4 cup extra-virgin olive oil
- 2 tbsps. chopped fresh cilantro, for garnish
- 1/2 cup sour cream

Directions:
1. Combine the ingredients for the seasoning in a bowl. Stir to mix well.
2. Put the pork rounds in the bowl of seasoning mixture. Toss to coat well.
3. Pour the olive oil into a nonstick skillet, and heat over medium-high heat.

4. Arrange the pork in the singer layer in the skillet and fry for 20 minutes or until an instant-read thermometer inserted in the center of the pork registers at least 145°F (63°C). Flip the pork rounds halfway through the cooking time. You may need to work in batches to avoid overcrowding.

5. Transfer the pork rounds onto a large platter, and top with cilantro and sour cream, then serve warm.

Nutrition for Total Servings:
- **Calories:** 289
- **Fat:** 23.2g
- **Carbs:** 2.8g
- **Protein:** 17.2g

Hot Pork and Bell Pepper in Lettuce

Preparation time: 15 minutes
Cooking time: 20 minutes
Servings: 4
Ingredients:
Sauce:

- 1 tbsp. fish sauce
- 1 tbsp. rice vinegar
- 1 tbsp. almond flour
- 1 tsp. coconut aminos
- 1 tbsp. granulated erythritol
- 2 tbsps. coconut oil

Pork filling:

- 2 tbsps. sesame oil, divided
- 1 pound (454 g) ground pork
- 1 tsp. fresh ginger, peeled and grated
- 1 tsp. garlic, minced
- 1 red bell pepper, deseeded and thinly sliced
- 1 scallion, white and green parts, thinly sliced
- 8 large romaine or Boston lettuce leaves

Directions:

1. Make the sauce: Combine the ingredients for the sauce in a bowl. Set aside until ready to use.
2. Make the pork filling: In a nonstick skillet, warm a tbsp. sesame oil over medium-high heat.
3. Add the sauté the ground pork for 8 minutes or until lightly browned, then pour the sauce over and keep cooking for 4 minutes more or until the sauce has lightly thickened.
4. Transfer the pork onto a platter and set aside until ready to use.
5. Clean the skillet with paper towels, then warm the remaining sesame oil over medium-high heat.
6. Add and sauté the ginger and garlic for 3 minutes or until fragrant.
7. Add and sauté the sliced bell pepper and scallion for an additional 5 minutes or until fork-tender.
8. Lower the heat, and move the pork back to the skillet. Stir to combine well.
9. Divide and arrange the pork filling over four lettuce leaves and serve hot.

Nutrition for Total Servings:

- **Calories:** 385
- **Fat:** 31.1g
- **Carbs:** 5.8g
- **Protein:** 20.1g

Italian Sausage, Zucchini, Eggplant, and Tomato Ratatouille

Preparation time: 15 minutes
Cooking time: 45 minutes
Servings: 4
Ingredients:

- 3 tbsps. extra-virgin olive oil
- 1 pound (454 g) Italian sausage meat (sweet or hot)
- 2 zucchini, diced
- 1 red bell pepper, diced
- 1/2 eggplant, cut into 1/2-inch cubes
- 1 tbsp. garlic, minced
- 1/2 red onion, chopped
- 1 tbsp. balsamic vinegar
- 1 (15-ounce/425-g) can low-sodium tomatoes, diced
- 1 tbsp. fresh basil, chopped
- Red pepper flakes, to taste
- 2 teaspoons chopped fresh oregano, for garnish
- Salt & freshly ground black pepper, to taste

Directions:

1. Add the olive oil in a stock pot, and warm over medium-high heat, then add and sauté the Italian sausage meat for 7 minutes or until lightly browned.
2. Add the zucchini, bell pepper, eggplant, garlic, and onion to the pot and sauté for 10 minutes or until tender.
3. Fold in the balsamic vinegar, tomatoes, basil, and red pepper flakes. Stir to combine well, then bring to a boil.
4. Turn down the heat to low. Simmer the mixture for 25 minutes or until the vegetables are entirely softened.
5. Sprinkle with oregano, salt, and black pepper. Stir to mix well, then serve warm.

Nutrition for Total Servings:

- **Calories:** 431
- **Fat**: 33.2g
- **Carbs**: 11.8g
- **Protein:** 21.2g

Bacon, Beef, and Pecan Patties

Preparation time: 10 minutes
Cooking time: 15 minutes
Servings: 8
Ingredients:
- 1/4 cup chopped onion
- 1/4 cup ground pecans
- 1 large egg
- 8 ounces (227 g) bacon, chopped
- 1 pound (454 g) grass-fed ground beef
- Salt & freshly ground black pepper, to taste
- 1 tbsp. extra-virgin olive oil

Directions:
1. Now, preheat the oven to 450°F (235°C). Line a baking sheet with parchment paper.
2. Whisk the ingredients, except for the olive oil, in a bowl.
3. Grease your hands with olive oil, and shape the mixture into 8 patties with your hands.
4. Arrange patties on a baking sheet and bake in the preheated oven for 20 min or until a meat thermometer inserted in the center of the patties reads at least 165°F (74°C). Flip patties halfway through cooking time.
5. Remove the cooked patties from the oven and serve warm.

TIP: You can serve the patties with homemade sauces or store-bought burger toppings for more and different flavors.

Nutrition for Total Servings:
- **Calories:** 318
- **Fat**: 27.2g
- **Carbs:** 1.1g
- **Protein**: 18.1g

Lemony Anchovy Butter with Steaks

Preparation time: 15 minutes
Cooking time: 10 minutes
Servings: 4
Ingredients:
Anchovy butter:

- 4 anchovies packed in oil, drained and minced
- 1/2 tsp. freshly squeezed lemon juice
- 1/4 cup unsalted butter, at room temperature
- 1 tsp. minced garlic
- 4 (4-ounce/113-g) rib-eye steaks
- Salt & freshly ground black pepper, to taste

Directions:

1. Make the anchovy butter: Combine the anchovies, lemon juice, butter, and garlic in a bowl. Stir to mix well, then arrange the bowl into the refrigerator to chill until ready to use.
2. Preheat the grill to medium-high heat.
3. Rub the steaks with salt and black pepper on a clean work surface.
4. Arrange the seasoned steaks on the grill grates and grill for 10 minutes or until medium-rare. Flip steaks halfway through cooking time.
5. Allow the steaks to cool for 10 minutes. Transfer the steaks onto four plates, and spread the anchovy butter on top, then serve warm.

TIP: To make this a complete meal, you can serve it with spicy asparagus. They also taste great paired with fresh cucumber salad.
Nutrition for Total Servings:

- **Calories:** 447
- **Fat:** 38.1g
- **Carbs**: 0g
- **Protein**: 26.1g

Zucchini Carbonara

Preparation time: 10 minutes
Cooking time: 15 minutes
Servings: 6
Ingredients:

- 8 chopped bacon slices
- 2 large eggs
- 4 large egg yolks
- 1/2 cup heavy whipping cream
- 2 tbsps. chopped fresh basil
- 2 tbsps. chopped fresh parsley
- Salt & freshly ground black pepper, to taste
- 1 tbsp. minced garlic
- 1/2 cup dry white wine
- 4 medium zucchini, spiralized

Directions:

1. In a nonstick skillet, cook the bacon for 6 minutes or until it curls and buckle. Flip bacon halfway through cooking time.
2. Meanwhile, whisk together the eggs, egg yolks, cream, basil, parsley, salt, & black pepper in a large bowl. Set aside.
3. Add the garlic to the skillet and sauté for 3 minutes until fragrant, then pour the dry white wine over and cook for an additional 2 minutes for deglazing.
4. Turn down the heat to low, add and sauté the spiralized zucchini for 2 minutes.
5. Pour egg mixture into skillet and toss for 4 minutes or until the mixture is thickened and coat the spiralized zucchini.
6. Transfer to a platter

TIP: To make this a complete meal, you can serve it with lemony radicchio salad. They also taste great paired with braised fennel and shallots.

Nutrition for Total Servings:

- **Calories:** 332
- **Fat:** 26.2g
- **Carbs:** 6.9g
- **Protein:** 19.1g

Mushroom, Spinach, and Onion Stuffed Meatloaf

Preparation time: 20 minutes
Cooking time: 1 hour
Servings: 8
Ingredients:

- 3 tbsps. extra-virgin olive oil
- 17 ounces (482 g) ground beef
- 2 teaspoons ground cumin
- 2 garlic cloves, granulated
- Salt & freshly ground black pepper, to taste
- 1/4 cup mushrooms, diced
- 1/2 cup spinach
- 1/4 cup onions, diced
- 1/4 cup green onions, diced

Directions:

1. Now, preheat your oven 350°F (180°C). Coat a meatloaf pan with olive oil.
2. Combine 1 pound (454 g) ground beef, cumin, garlic, salt, and black pepper in a large bowl. Pour the mixture into the meatloaf pan.
3. Make a well in the center of the beef mixture. Put the mushrooms, spinach, and onions in the well, then cover them with the remaining 1 ounce (28 g) ground beef.
4. Place the meatloaf pan into the preheated oven and bake for 1 hour until cooked through.
5. Remove meatloaf from oven and slice to serve.

TIP: To gift this dish with more flavor. You can serve it with homemade spicy or sour sauces, or store-bought toppings.

Nutrition for Total Servings:

- **Calories:** 254
- **Fat:** 20.2g
- **Carbs**: 1.4g
- **Protein:** 15.3g

Italian Flavor Herbed Pork Chops

Preparation time: 10 minutes
Cooking time: 20 minutes
Servings: 4
Ingredients:
- 2 tbsps. melted butter, plus for coating
- 2 tbsps. Italian seasoning
- 2 tbsps. olive oil
- Salt & freshly ground black pepper, to taste (if no salt or pepper in the Italian seasoning)
- 4 pork chops, boneless
- 2 tbsps. fresh Italian leaf parsley, chopped

Directions:
1. Now, preheat the oven to 350°F (180°C). Grease a baking dish with melted butter.
2. Combine the Italian seasoning, butter, olive oil, salt, and black pepper in a large bowl. Dredge each pork chop into the bowl to coat well.
3. Arrange the pork chops onto the baking dish, and spread the fresh parsley on top of each chop.
4. Bake in preheated oven for 20 mins. Or until cooked through. An instant-read thermometer inserted in the middle of the pork chops should register at least 145°F (63°C).
5. Transfer the pork chops from the oven and serve warm.

TIP: To make this a complete meal, you can serve it with roasted broccoli. They also taste great paired with creamy spinach and dill.

Nutrition for Total Servings:
- **Calories:** 335
- **Fat:** 23.4g
- **Carbs**: 0g
- **Protein:** 30.9g

Braised Beef Shanks and Dry Red Wine

Preparation time: 10 minutes
Cooking time: 8 hours
Servings: 6
Ingredients:
- 2 tbsps. olive oil
- 2 pounds (907 g) beef shanks
- 2 cups dry red wine
- 3 cups beef stock
- 1 sprig of fresh rosemary
- 5 garlic cloves, finely chopped
- 1 onion, finely chopped
- Salt & freshly ground black pepper, to taste

Directions:
1. In a nonstick skillet, warm olive oil over medium-high heat.
2. Put the beef shanks into the skillet and fry for 5 to 10 minutes until well browned. Flip the beef shanks halfway through. Set aside.
3. Pour the dry red wine into the skillet & bring it to a simmer.
4. Coat the insert of the slow cooker with olive oil.
5. Add the cooked beef shanks, dry red wine, beef stock, rosemary, garlic, onion, salt, and black pepper to the slow cooker. Stir to mix well.
6. Put slow cooker lid on & cook on LOW for 8 hours until the beef shanks are fork-tender.
7. Remove from the slow cooker & serve hot.

TIP: To make this a complete meal, you can serve it with roasted cauliflower. They also taste great paired with tomato and herb salad.

Nutrition for Total Servings:
- **Calories:** 315
- **Fat:** 11g
- **Carbs**: 4g
- **Protein:** 50g

Beef, Eggplant, Zucchini, and Baby Spinach Lasagna

Preparation time: 10 minutes
Cooking time: 4 hours
Servings: 8
Ingredients:
- 3 tbsps. olive oil, plus for greasing the slow cooker
- 5 garlic cloves, finely chopped
- 1 onion, finely chopped
- 2 pounds (907 g) beef, minced
- 2 teaspoons dried mixed herbs (oregano, rosemary, thyme)
- 4 tomatoes, chopped
- Salt & freshly ground black pepper, to taste
- 1 large eggplant, cut into round slices crosswise
- 2 large zucchinis, cut into slices lengthwise
- 2 cups baby spinach leaves

Directions:
1. Warm the olive oil in a nonstick skillet over medium-high heat.
2. Add and sauté the garlic and onions for 3 minutes or until the onions are translucent.
3. Add and sauté the beef for 3 more minutes until lightly browned.
4. Add the dried mixed herbs and tomatoes over the beef, and season with salt and black pepper. Sauté for 5 minutes to combine well.
5. Grease the slow cooker with olive oil.
6. Make the lasagna: Spread a layer of beef mixture on the bottom of the slow cooker, and top the beef mixture with a layer of eggplant slices, then spread another layer of beef mixture, and then put on a layer of zucchini slices, after that, top the zucchini slices with a layer of beef mixture, and on the beef mixture, spread a layer of baby spinach leaves, and finally, a layer of beef mixture.
7. Combine the salt and black pepper in a large bowl. Put the slow cooker lid on and bake on HIGH for 4 hours.
8. Remove the hot lasagna from the slow cooker and slice to serve.

N You can use different vegetable slices to replace the eggplant, zucchinis, or baby spinach leaves, such as tomato slices and broccoli slices.

Nutrition for Total Servings:
- **Calories:** 397
- **Fat:** 22.0g
- **Carbs:** 10.5g
- **Protein:** 40.8g

Lamb and Tomato Curry

Preparation time: 10 minutes
Cooking time: 8 hours
Servings: 8
Ingredients:

- 3 tbsps. olive oil, plus for greasing the slow cooker
- 2 1/2 lb. (1.1 kg) boneless lamb shoulder, cubed
- 4 tbsps. curry paste
- 5 garlic cloves, finely chopped
- 2 onions, roughly chopped
- Salt & freshly ground black pepper, to taste
- 1 lamb stock cube
- 2 tomatoes, chopped
- 2 1/2 cups unsweetened oat milk
- 1 cup of water
- Fresh coriander, roughly chopped, for garnish
- Full-fat Greek yogurt, to serve

Directions:

1. Warm the olive oil in a nonstick skillet over medium-high heat.
2. Add and sear the lamb shoulder for 3 minutes until browned on both sides.
3. Grease the slow cooker with olive oil.
4. Place the cooked lamb into the slow cooker, and add the curry paste, garlic, onions, salt, and black pepper. Toss to coat the lamb well.
5. Add the stock cube, tomatoes, oat milk, and water to the slow cooker. Stir to mix well.
6. Put the slow cooker lid on & cook on LOW for 8 hours.
7. Transfer the lamb curry to a large plate, and spread the coriander and yogurt on top to serve.

TIP: To make this a complete meal, you can serve it with Indian raita, cucumber salad, and naan.

Nutrition for Total Servings:

- **Calories:** 406
- **Fat:** 28.2g
- **Carbs:** 10.5g
- **Protein:** 31.6g

Garlicky Lamb Leg with Rosemary

Preparation time: 15 minutes
Cooking time: 30 minutes
Servings: 8
Ingredients:

- 3 tbsps. extra-virgin olive oil
- 4 pounds (1.8 kg) boneless leg of lamb
- Salt & freshly ground black pepper, to taste
- 2 tbsps. chopped rosemary
- 1 tbsp. garlic
- 2 cups of water

Directions:

1. Warm the olive oil in a nonstick skillet over medium-high heat.
2. Add lamb leg to the skillet, and sprinkle with salt and black pepper. Sear for 3 minutes until browned on both sides.
3. Remove the lamb leg from the skillet to a platter. Allow to cool few minutes, then rub with rosemary and garlic.
4. Pour the water into a pressure cooker with a steamer, then arrange the lamb leg on the steamer.
5. Put the pressure cooker lid on and cook for 30 minutes.
6. Release the pressure, and remove the lamb leg from the pressure cooker. Allow to cool 10 minutes & slice to serve.

TIP: If you think the taste of this recipe is a little plain, you can try to top the lamb leg with your secret glaze or homemade sauce to gift more flavor to the lamb leg.

Nutrition for Total Servings:

- **Calories:** 366
- **Fat:** 16.2g
- **Carbs:** 1.2g
- **Protein:** 51.1g

Lamb Chops with Dry Red Wine

Preparation time: 10 minutes
Cooking time: 40 minutes
Servings: 4
Ingredients:
- 1 tbsp. olive oil
- 1 garlic clove, minced
- 1/2 onion, sliced
- 1 pound (454 g) lamb chops
- 1/2 tsp. mint
- 1/2 tbsp. sage
- Salt & freshly ground black pepper, to taste
- 1/4 cup dry red wine
- 1 cup of water

Directions:
1. Warm the olive oil in a nonstick skillet over medium-high heat.
2. Sauté the garlic and onion in the skillet for 3 minutes or until the onion is translucent.
3. Arrange the lamb chops on a clean work surface and rub with mint, sage, salt, and black pepper on both sides.
4. Add the lamb chops in the skillet and cook for 6 minutes until lightly browned. Flip the chops halfway through. Set aside.
5. Pour the dry red wine and water into the skillet. Bring to a boil, then cook until it reduces to half.
6. Add the cooked lamb chops back to the skillet. Lower the heat, & simmer for 30 minutes.
7. Remove them from the skillet and serve hot.

TIP: If you think the taste of this recipe is a little plain, you can try to top the lamb chops with your secret glaze or homemade sauce to gift more flavor to the lamb chops.

Nutrition for Total Servings:
- **Calories**: 341
- **Fat:** 29.8g
- **Carbs:** 3.6g
- **Protein:** 14.6g

Pork with Veggies

Preparation time: 15 minutes
Cooking time: 15 minutes
Servings: 5
Ingredients:

- 1 quid pork loin, cut into thin strips
- 2 tbsps. olive oil, divided
- 1 tsp. garlic, minced
- 1 tsp. fresh ginger, minced
- 2 tbsps. low-sodium soy sauce
- 1 tbsp. fresh lemon juice
- 1 tsp. sesame oil
- 1 tbsp. granulated erythritol
- 1 tsp. arrowroot star
- 10 ounces' broccoli florets
- 1 carrot, peeled and sliced
- 1 big red bell pepper, seeded and cut into strips
- 2 scallions, cut into 2-inch pieces

Directions:

1. In a bowl, mix well pork strips, 1/2 tbsp. of olive oil, garlic, and ginger.

For the sauce:

1. Add the soy sauce, lemon juice, sesame oil, Swerve, and arrowroot starch in a small bowl and mix well.
2. Preheat the oven remaining olive oil in a big nonstick wok over high heat and sear the pork strips for about 3–4 minutes or until cooked through.
3. With a slotted spoon, transfer the pork into a bowl.
4. In the same wok, add the carrot and cook for about 2–3 minutes.
5. Add the broccoli, bell pepper, and scallion, and cook, covered for about 1–2 minutes.
6. Stir the cooked pork, sauce, and stir fry, and cook for about 3–5 minutes or until the desired doneness, stirring occasionally.
7. Remove from the heat and serve.

Nutrition for Total Servings:

- **Calories:** 268 Cal
- **Fat:** 18 g
- **Carbs**: 7 g
- **Protein**: 8 g

Pork Taco Bake

Preparation time: 15 minutes
Cooking time: 60 minutes
Servings: 6
Ingredients:
Crust:

- 3 organic eggs
- 1/2 tsp. taco seasoning
- 1/3 cup heavy cream

Topping:

- 1 pound lean ground pork
- 4 ounces canned chopped green chilies
- 1/4 cup sugar-free tomato sauce
- 3 teaspoons taco seasoning
- 1/4 cup fresh basil leaves

Directions:

1. Now, preheat the oven to 375°F.
2. Lightly grease a 13x9-inch baking dish.
3. For the crust: In a bowl, add the eggs, and beat until well combined and smooth.
4. Add the taco seasoning and heavy cream, and mix well.
5. Bake for about 25–30 minutes.
6. Remove baking dish from oven and set aside for about 5 minutes.
7. Meanwhile, for the topping: Heat a large nonstick wok over medium-high heat and cook the pork for about 8–10 minutes.
8. Drain the excess grease from the wok.
9. Stir in the green chilies, tomato sauce, and taco seasoning, and remove from the heat.
10. Place the pork mixture evenly over the crust.
11. Bake for about 18–20 minutes or until bubbly.
12. Remove from the oven and set aside for about 5 minutes.
13. Cut into desired size slices and serve with the garnishing of basil leaves.

Nutrition for Total Servings:

- **Calories:** 198 Cal
- **Fat:** 12 g
- **Carbs:** 8 g
- **Protein:** 19 g

Creamy Pork Stew

Preparation time: 15 minutes
Cooking time: 95 minutes
Servings: 8
Ingredients:
- 3 tbsps. unsalted butter
- 2 1/2 pounds boneless pork ribs, cut into 3/4-inch cubes
- 1 large yellow onion, chopped
- 4 garlic cloves, crushed
- 1 1/2 cups homemade chicken broth
- 2 (10-ounce) cans of sugar-free diced tomatoes
- 2 teaspoons dried oregano
- 1 tsp. ground cumin
- Salt, to taste
- 2 tbsps. fresh lime juice
- 1/2 cup sour cream

Directions:
1. In a large heavy-bottomed pan, dissolve the butter over medium-high heat and cook the pork, onions, and garlic for about 4–5 min. Or until browned.
2. Add the broth and with a wooden spoon, scrape up the browned bits.
3. Add the tomatoes, oregano, cumin, and salt, and stir to combine well
4. Adjust the temperature to medium-low and simmer, covered for about 1 1/2 hours.
5. Stir in the sour cream and lime juice and remove from the heat.
6. Serve hot.

Nutrition for Total Servings:
- **Calories:** 182 Cal
- **Fat:** 18 g
- **Carbs:** 9 g
- **Protein:** 18 g

Creamy Basil Baked Sausage

Preparation time: 5 minutes
Cooking time: 30 minutes
Servings: 2
Ingredients:

- 3 lb. of Italian sausage - pork/turkey or chicken
- ¼ cup of heavy cream
- ¼ cup of basil pesto
- 80 g mozzarella

Directions:

1. Set the oven to 400°F.
2. Lightly spritz a casserole dish with cooking oil spray. Add the sausage to the dish and bake for 30 minutes.
3. Combine the heavy cream, pesto
4. Pour the sauce over the casserole
5. Bake for another 10 minutes. The sausage should reach 160°Fahrenheit in the center when checked with a meat thermometer.
6. You can also broil for 3 minutes to brown the cheesy layer.

Nutrition for Total Servings:

- **Calories:** 298 Cal
- **Fat:** 17 g
- **Carbs:** 4 g
- **Protein:** 9 g

Chicken Pan-Grilled With Chorizo Confetti

Preparation time: 5 minutes
Cooking time: 30 minutes
Servings: 4
Ingredients:

- 4 (6-ounce) skinless, boneless chicken bosom parts
- 1/2 tsp. genuine salt, isolated
- 1/4 tsp. newly ground dark pepper
- Cooking splash
- 1/4 cup Mexican pork chorizo, housings expelled
- 1/4 cup cut onion
- 2 carrots, diced
- 1/4 cup diced yellow ringer pepper
- 1/4 cup diced red chime pepper
- 2 tbsps. diced green chime pepper
- 1/4 cup unsalted chicken stock
- 1 tbsp. cleaved new cilantro Green Salad with Crostini.

Directions:

1. Warmth a flame broil skillet over medium-high warmth.
2. Sprinkle chicken with 1/4 tsp. salt and pepper.
3. Coat dish with cooking splash.
4. Add chicken to the dish; cook 6 minutes on each side or until done.
5. While chicken cooks heat a huge skillet over medium-high warmth. Include chorizo; cook 1 moment, mixing to disintegrate.
6. Include staying 1/4 tsp. salt, onion, and carrot; cook 2 minutes, blending infrequently.
7. Include chime peppers; cook 1 moment or until fresh delicate. Include stock; cook 2 minutes or until fluid nearly vanishes, scratching container to slacken sautéed bits.
8. Spoon chorizo blend over chicken; top with cilantro.

Nutrition for Total Servings:

- **Calories:** 190 Cal
- **Fat:** 22 g
- **Carbs:** 5 g
- **Protein:** 12 g
- **Fiber:** 3 g

Italian Pork Dish

Preparation time: 15 minutes
Cooking time: 15 minutes
Servings: 6
Ingredients:

- 2 lbs. pork tenderloins, cut into 1 1/2-inch each piece
- 1/4 cup of. almond flour
- 1 tsp. garlic salt
- Freshly ground black pepper, to taste
- 2 tbsps. butter
- 1/2 cup of homemade chicken broth
- 1/3 cup of balsamic vinegar
- 1 tbsp. capers
- 2 tsps. fresh lemon zest, grated finely

Directions:

1. In a large bowl, add pork pieces, flour, garlic salt, and black pepper and toss to coat well.
2. Remove pork pieces from the bowl and shake off excess flour mixture.
3. In a large skillet, melt butter over medium-high heat and cook the pork pieces for about 2-3 minutes per side.
4. Add broth & vinegar and bring to a gentle boil.
5. Reduce the heat to medium and simmer for about 3-4 minutes.
6. With a slotted spoon, transfer the pork pieces onto a plate.
7. In the same skillet, add the capers and lemon zest and simmer for about 3-5 minutes or until the desired thickness of the sauce.
8. Pour sauce over pork pieces and serve.

Nutrition for Total Servings:

- **Calories**: 484 Cal
- **Fat: 19** g
- **Carbs**: 8 g
- **Protein**: 10 g

Classic Pork Tenderloin

Preparation time: 15 minutes
Cooking time: 35 minutes
Servings: 4
Ingredients:

- 8 bacon slices
- 2 lb. pork tenderloin
- 1 tsp. dried oregano, crushed
- 1 tsp. dried basil, crushed
- 1 tbsp. garlic powder
- 1 tsp. seasoned salt
- 3 tbsp. butter

Directions:

1. Now, preheat the oven to 400°F.
2. Heat a large ovenproof skillet over medium-high heat and cook the bacon for about 6-7 minutes.
3. Transfer the bacon onto a paper towel-lined plate to drain.
4. Then, wrap the pork tenderloin with bacon slices and secure it with toothpicks.
5. With a sharp knife, slice the tenderloin between each bacon slice to make a medallion.
6. In a bowl, mix together the dried herbs, garlic powder and seasoned salt.
7. Now, coat the medallion with herb mixture.
8. With a paper towel, wipe out the skillet.
9. In the same skillet, melt the butter over medium-high heat and cook the pork medallion for about 4 minutes per side.
10. Now, transfer the skillet into the oven.
11. Roast for about 17-20 minutes.
12. Remove the wok from the oven and let it cool slightly before cutting.
13. Cut the tenderloin into desired size slices and serve.

Nutrition for Total Servings:

- **Calories**: 471
- **Carbs**: 1g
- **Protein**: 53.5g
- **Fat:** 26.6g

The Signature Italian Pork Dish

Preparation time: 15 minutes
Cooking time: 15 minutes
Servings: 6
Ingredients:

- 2 lb. pork tenderloins, cut into 1 1/2-inch piece
- 1/4 C. almond flour
- 1 tsp. garlic salt
- Freshly ground black pepper, to taste
- 2 tbsp. butter
- 1/2 C. homemade chicken broth
- 1/3 C. balsamic vinegar
- 1 tbsp. capers
- 2 tsp. fresh lemon zest, grated finely

Directions:

1. In a large bowl, add pork pieces, flour, garlic salt and black pepper and toss to coat well.
2. Remove pork pieces from the bowl and shake off excess flour mixture.
3. In a large skillet, melt the butter over medium-high heat and cook the pork pieces for about 2-3 minutes per side.
4. Add broth & vinegar and bring to a gentle boil.
5. Reduce the heat to medium and simmer for about 3-4 minutes.
6. With a slotted spoon, transfer the pork pieces onto a plate.
7. In the same skillet, add the capers and lemon zest and simmer for about 3-5 minutes or until the desired thickness of the sauce.
8. Pour sauce over pork pieces and serve.

Nutrition for Total Servings:

- **Calories:** 373
- **Carbs:** 1.8g
- **Protein:** 46.7g
- **Fat:** 18.6g

Spiced Pork Tenderloin

Preparation time: 15 minutes
Cooking time: 18 minutes
Servings: 6
Ingredients:

- 2 tsp. fennel seeds
- 2 tsp. coriander seeds
- 2 tsp. caraway seeds
- 1 tsp. cumin seeds
- 1 bay leaf
- Salt & freshly ground black pepper, to taste
- 2 tbsp. fresh dill, chopped
- 2 (1-lb.) pork tenderloins, trimmed

Directions:

1. For the spice rub: in a spice grinder, add the seeds and bay leaf and grind until finely powdered.
2. Add the salt and black pepper and mix.
3. In a small bowl, reserve 2 tbsp. Of spice rub.
4. In another small bowl, mix the remaining spice rub, and dill.
5. Place 1 tenderloin over a piece of plastic wrap.
6. With a sharp knife, slice through the meat to within 1/2-inch of the opposite side.
7. Now, open the tenderloin like a book.
8. Cover with another plastic wrap and with a meat pounder, gently pound into 1/2-inch thickness.
9. Repeat with the remaining tenderloin.
10. Remove the plastic wrap and spread half of the dill mixture over the center of each tenderloin.
11. Roll each tenderloin like a cylinder.
12. With a kitchen string, tightly tie each roll at several places.
13. Rub each roll with the reserved spice rub generously.
14. With 1 plastic wrap, wrap each roll and refrigerate for at least 4-6 hours.
15. Preheat the grill to medium-high heat. Grease the grill grate.
16. Remove the plastic wrap from tenderloins.
17. Place tenderloins onto the grill and cook for about 14-18 minutes, flipping.
18. Remove from the grill and place tenderloins onto a cutting board and with a piece of foil, cover each tenderloin for at least 5-10 minutes before slicing.
19. With a sharp knife, cut the tenderloins into desired size slices and serve.

Nutrition for Total Servings:

- **Calories:** 313
- **Carbs:** 1.4g
- **Protein:** 45.7g
- **Fat:** 12.6g

Sticky Pork Ribs

Preparation time: 15 minutes
Cooking time: 2 hours 34 minutes
Servings: 9
Ingredients:
- 1/4 cup erythritol
- 1 tbsp. garlic powder
- 1 tbsp. Paprika
- 1/2 tsp. red chili powder
- 4 lb. pork ribs, membrane removed
- Salt & freshly ground black pepper, to taste
- 1 1/2 tsp. liquid smoke
- 1 1/2 C. sugar-free BBQ sauce

Directions:
1. Now, preheat the oven to 300°F. Line a large baking sheet with 2 layers of foil, shiny side out.
2. In a bowl, add the Erythritol, garlic powder, paprika and chili powder and mix well.
3. Season the ribs with salt and black pepper and then, coat with the liquid smoke.
4. Now, rub the ribs with the Erythritol mixture.
5. Arrange the ribs onto the prepared baking sheet, meaty side down.
6. Arrange 2 layers of foil on top of ribs and then, roll and crimp edges tightly.
7. Bake for about 2-2 1/2 hours or until the desired doneness.
8. Remove baking sheet from oven and place the ribs onto a cutting board.
9. Now, set the oven to broiler.
10. With a sharp knife, and then cut the ribs into serving sized portions and evenly coat with the barbecue sauce.
11. Arrange the ribs onto a broiler pan, bony side up.
12. Broil for about 1-2 minutes per side.
13. Remove from the oven and serve hot.

Nutrition for Total Servings:
- **Calories**: 530
- **Carbs:** 2.8g
- **Protein:** 60.4g
- **Fat**: 40.3g

Valentine's Day Dinner

Preparation time: 15 minutes
Cooking time: 35 minutes
Servings: 4
Ingredients:
- 1 tbsp. olive oil
- 4 large boneless rib pork chops
- 1 tsp. salt
- 1 cup cremini mushrooms, chopped roughly
- 3 tbsp. yellow onion, chopped finely
- 2 tbsp. fresh rosemary, chopped
- 1/3 cup homemade chicken broth
- 1 tbsp. unsalted butter
- 2/3 cup heavy cream
- 2 tbsp. sour cream

Directions:
1. Now, preheat the oven oil in a large skillet over medium heat and sear the chops with the salt for about 3-4 minutes or until browned completely.
2. With a slotted spoon, transfer the pork chops onto a plate and set aside.
3. In the same skillet, add mushrooms, onion and rosemary and sauté for about 3 minutes.
4. Stir in the cooked chops, broth and bring to a boil.
5. Reduce heat to low & cook, covered for about 20 minutes.
6. With a slotted spoon, transfer the pork chops onto a plate and set aside.
7. In the skillet, stir in the butter until melted.
8. Add the heavy cream and sour cream and stir until smooth.
9. Stir in the cooked pork chops and cook for about 2-3 minutes or until heated completely.
10. Serve hot.

Nutrition for Total Servings:
- **Calories:** 400
- **Carbs:** 3.6g
- **Protein:** 46.3g
- **Fat:** 21.6g

South East Asian Steak Platter

Preparation time: 15 minutes
Cooking time: 20 minutes
Servings: 4
Ingredients:

- 14 oz. grass-fed sirloin steak, trimmed and cut into thin strips
- Freshly ground black pepper, to taste
- 2 tbsp. olive oil, divided
- 1 small yellow onion, chopped
- 2 garlic cloves, minced
- 1 Serrano pepper, seeded and chopped finely
- 3 C. broccoli florets
- 3 tbsp. low-sodium soy sauce
- 2 tbsp. fresh lime juice

Directions:

1. Season steak with black pepper.
2. In a large skillet, heat 1 tbsp. Of the oil over medium heat and cook the steak for about 6-8 minutes or until browned from all sides.
3. Transfer the steak onto a plate.
4. In the same skillet, heat remaining oil and sauté onion for about 3-4 minutes.
5. Add the garlic and Serrano pepper and sauté for about 1 minute.
6. Add broccoli and stir fry for about 2-3 minutes.
7. Stir in cooked beef, soy sauce and lime juice and cook for about 3-4 minutes.
8. Serve hot.

Nutrition for Total Servings:

- **Calories**: 282
- **Carbs**: 7.6g
- **Protein**: 33.1g
- **Fat:** 13.5g

Pesto Flavored Steak

Preparation time: 15 minutes
Cooking time: 17 minutes
Servings: 4
Ingredients:
- 1/4 cup fresh oregano, chopped
- 1 1/2 tbsp. garlic, minced
- 1 tbsp. fresh lemon peel, grated
- 1/2 tsp. red pepper flakes and crushed
- Salt & freshly ground black pepper, to taste
- 1 lb. (1-inch thick) grass-fed boneless beef top sirloin steak
- 1 cup pesto

Directions:
1. Preheat gas grill to medium heat. Lightly, grease the grill grate.
2. In a bowl, add oregano, garlic, lemon peel, red pepper flakes, salt & black pepper & mix well.
3. Rub garlic mixture onto the steak evenly.
4. Place steak onto the grill and cook, covered for about 12-17 minutes, flipping occasionally.
5. Remove from the grill and place the steak onto a cutting board for about 5 minutes.
6. With a sharp knife, cut the steak into desired sized slices.
7. Divide the steak slices and pesto onto serving plates and serve

Nutrition for Total Servings:
- **Calories**: 226
- **Carbs:** 6.8g
- **Protein:** 40.5g
- **Fat:** 7.6g

Flawless Grilled Steak

Cooking time: 10 minutes
Preparation time: 21 minutes
Servings: 5
Ingredients:
- 1/2 tsp. dried thyme, crushed
- 1/2 tsp. dried oregano, crushed
- 1 tsp. red chili powder
- 1/2 tsp. ground cumin
- 1/4 tsp. garlic powder
- Salt & freshly ground black pepper, to taste
- 1 1/2 lb. grass-fed flank steak, trimmed

Directions:
1. In a large bowl, add the dried herbs and spices and mix well.
2. Add the steaks and rub with mixture generously.
3. Set aside for about 15-20 minutes.
4. Preheat the grill to medium heat. Grease the grill grate.
5. Place the steak onto the grill over medium coals and cook for about 17-21 minutes, flipping once halfway through.
6. Remove the steak from the grill and place onto a cutting board for about 10 minutes before slicing.
7. With a sharp knife, and then cut the steak into desired sized slices.

Nutrition for Total Servings:
- **Calories:** 271
- **Carbs:** 0.7g
- **Protein**: 38.3g
- **Fat:** 11.8g

Beef and Pepper Kebabs

Preparation time: 30 minutes
Cooking time: 10 minutes
Servings: 2
Ingredients:
- 2 tbsps. olive oil
- 1 1/2 tbsp. balsamic vinegar
- 2 teaspoons of Dijon mustard
- Salt & pepper
- 8 ounces of beef sirloin, cut into 2-inch pieces
- 1 small red pepper, and then cut into chunks
- 1 small green pepper, and then cut into chunks

Directions:
1. Whisk the olive oil, balsamic vinegar, & mustard in a shallow dish.
2. Season the steak with salt and pepper, then toss in the marinade.
3. Let marinate for 30 minutes, then slide onto skewers with the peppers.
4. Preheat a grill pan to high heat and grease with cooking spray.
5. Cook the kebabs for 2 to 3 min on each side until the beef is done.

Nutrition for Total Servings:
- **Calories:** 365
- **Fat:** 21.5g
- **Protein:** 35.5g
- **Carbs:** 6.5g

Chinese Pork Bowl

Preparation time: 5 minutes
Cooking time: 15 minutes
Servings: 4
Ingredients:

- 1 1/4 pounds pork belly, cut into bite-size pieces
- 2 Tbsp. tamari soy sauce
- 1 Tbsp. rice vinegar
- 2 cloves garlic, smashed
- 3 oz. butter
- 1 pound Brussels sprouts, rinsed, trimmed, halved or quartered
- 1/2 leek, chopped
- Salt and ground black pepper, to taste

Directions:

1. Fry the pork over medium-high heat until it is starting to turn golden brown.
2. Combine the garlic cloves, butter, and Brussels sprouts. Add to the pan, whisk well and cook until the sprouts turn golden brown.
3. Stir the soy sauce & rice vinegar together and pour the sauce into the pan.
4. Sprinkle with salt and pepper.
5. Top with chopped leek.

Nutrition for Total Servings:

- **Carbs:** 7 g
- **Fat:** 97 g
- **Protein:** 19 g
- **Calories:** 993

Flavor Packed Pork Loin

Preparation time: 15 minutes
Cooking time: 60 minutes
Servings: 6
Ingredients:

- 1/3 cup of low-sodium soy sauce
- 1/4 cup of fresh lemon juice
- 2 tsps. fresh lemon zest, grated
- 1 tbsp. fresh thyme, finely chopped
- 2 tbsps. fresh ginger, grated
- 2 garlic cloves, chopped finely
- 2 tbsps. Erythritol
- Freshly ground black pepper, to taste
- 1/2 tsp. cayenne pepper
- 2 lbs. boneless pork loin

Directions:

1. For pork marinade: in a large baking dish, add all the ingredients except pork loin and mix until well combined.
2. Add pork loin and coat with the marinade generously.
3. Refrigerate for about 24 hours.
4. Now, preheat the oven to 400°F.
5. Remove pork loin from marinade and arrange it into a baking dish.
6. Cover the baking dish and bake for about 1 hour.
7. Remove from the oven and place the pork loin onto a cutting board.
8. With a piece of foil, cover each loin for at least 10 minutes before slicing.
9. With a sharp knife, cut the pork loin into desired size slices and serve.

Nutrition for Total Servings:

- **Calories:** 230 Cal
- **Fat:** 29 g
- **Carbs**: 4 g
- **Protein:** 10 g

Keto Breakfast Cups

Preparation time: 15 minutes
Cooking time: 40 minutes
Servings: 12
Ingredients:

- 2 lbs. ground pork
- 1 tbsp. freshly chopped thyme
- 2 cloves garlic, minced
- 1/2 tsp. paprika
- 1/2 tsp. ground cumin
- 1 tsp. kosher salt
- Freshly ground black pepper
- 2 1/2 cups chopped fresh spinach
- 12 eggs
- 1 tbsp. freshly chopped chives

Directions:

1. Preheats the oven to 400°c. Combine the pork, thyme, garlic, paprika, cumin, and salt in a large bowl. Season with peppers.
2. Attach a small handful of pork to each tin of muffin well then press the sides to make a cup. Spinach Season with salt and pepper and crack an egg on top of each cup.
3. Bake for about 25 min, until eggs are set, and the pork is cooked through. Garnish and serve with chives.
4. Serve hot.

Nutrition for Total Servings:

- **Calories:** 418 Cal
- **Fat:** 30 g
- **Carbs:** 9 g
- **Protein:** 19 g

Keto Stuffed Cabbage

Preparation time: 15 minutes
Cooking time: 45 minutes
Servings: 12
Ingredients:
Sauce:

- 1 (14-oz.) can diced tomatoes
- 1 tbsp. apple cider vinegar
- 1/2 tsp. red pepper flakes
- 1 tsp. onion powder
- 1 tsp. garlic powder
- 1 tsp. dried oregano
- Kosher salt
- Freshly ground black pepper
- 1/4 cup of extra-virgin olive oil

Cabbage Rolls:

- 12 cabbage leaves
- 1 lb. ground beef
- 3/4 lb. ground pork
- 1 cup rice cauliflower
- 3 green onions, thinly sliced
- 1/4 cup of chopped parsley, plus for serving
- Freshly ground black pepper and salt

Directions:
Sauce:

1. Now, preheat the oven to 375°C. Puree tomatoes, in a blender, apple cider vinegar, red pepper flakes, onion powder, garlic powder and oregano; salt and pepper seasoning.
2. Heat oil in large, deep pan (or big pot) over medium heat. Add the pureed tomato sauce, bring to a simmer then lower to medium-low, and cook for 20 minutes until thickened slightly.

Cabbage Rolls:

1. Flinch the cabbage leaves in a large pot of boiling water until tender and flexible, around 1 minute set aside
2. For the filling: mix 1/2 c in a large bowl. Tomato sauce, meat from the farm, cauliflower rice, scallions, and parsley. Top with pepper and salt.
3. Put a thin layer of sauce on a large baking dish underneath. Slice the hard-triangular rib out of each cabbage leaf using a paring knife. Place approximately 1/3 cup filling in one end of each leaf, then roll up and tuck into the sides as you move. Layer rolls in a baking dish to seam-side-down on top of the sauce. Remaining spoon sauce over the cabbage rolls. Bake until the meat is properly cooked through and the internal temperature hits 150°F for 45 minutes to 55 minutes. Apply more parsley to garnish before serving.

Nutrition for Total Servings:

- **Calories:** 229 Cal
- **Fat**: 20 g
- **Carbs**: 3 g
- **Protein:** 19 g

Garlic Rosemary Pork Chops

Preparation time: 10 minutes
Cooking time: 30 minutes
Servings: 4
Ingredients:
- 4 pork loin chops
- Kosher salt
- Freshly ground black pepper
- 1 tbsp. freshly minced rosemary
- 2 cloves garlic, minced
- 1/2 cup (1 stick) butter, melted
- 1 tbsp. extra-virgin olive oil

Directions:
1. Now, preheat the oven to 375°F. Spice the pork with salt and pepper generously.
2. Mix the butter, rosemary, and garlic together in a small bowl. Set aside.
3. Heat olive oil over medium-high flame, then places pork chops in an oven-safe skillet. Sear for 4 minutes until crispy, flip over and cook for 4 minutes. Clean the pork with garlic butter, generously.
4. Place the bucket in the oven and cook for 10-12 minutes until cooked (145°F for medium). Serve with more butter over garlic.

Nutrition for Total Servings:
- **Calories:** 390 Cal
- **Fat:** 30 g
- **Carbs**: 6 g
- **Protein:** 19g

Chicken Parmesan

Preparation time: 20 minutes
Cooking time: 15 minutes
Servings: 4
Ingredients:

- 1/4 cup of avocado oil
- 1/4 cup of almond flour
- 3/4 cup of marinara sauce, sugar-free
- 2 eggs, beaten
- 2 tsps. Italian seasoning
- 3 oz. pork rinds, pulverized
- 4 lbs. chicken breasts, boneless & skinless
- Sea salt & pepper, to taste
- 1/3 cup parmesan cheese

Directions:

1. Now, preheat the oven to 450°Fahrenheit and grease a baking dish.
2. Place the beaten egg into one shallow dish. Place the almond flour in another. In a third dish, combine the pork rinds, parmesan, pepper, salt and Italian seasoning and mix well.
3. Pat the chicken breasts dry and pound them down to about 1/2" thick.
4. Dredge the chicken in the almond flour, then coat in egg, then coat in the crumb.
5. Heat a large sauté pan over medium-high heat and warm oil until shimmering.
6. Once the oil is hot, lay the breasts into the pan and do not move them until they've had a chance to cook. Cook for about two minutes, then flip as gently as possible (a fish spatula is perfect) then cook for two more. Remove the pan from the heat.
7. Place the breasts in the greased baking dish and top with marinara sauce Bake for about 10 minutes.
8. Serve!

Nutrition for Total Servings:

- **Calories:** 621 Cal
- **Fat:** 24 g
- **Carbs:** 6 g
- **Protein:** 14 g

Potluck Lamb Salad

Preparation time: 20 minutes
Cooking time: 10 minutes
Servings: 4
Ingredients:

- 2 tbsp. olive oil, divided
- 12 oz. grass-fed lamb leg steaks, trimmed
- 200 g halloumi
- Salt & freshly ground black pepper, to taste
- 2 jarred roasted red bell peppers, sliced thinly
- 2 cucumbers, cut into thin ribbons
- 3 C. fresh baby spinach
- 2 tbsp. balsamic vinegar

Directions:

1. In a skillet, heat 1 tbsp. Of the oil over medium-high heat and cook the lamb steaks for about 4-5 minutes per side or until desired doneness.
2. Transfer the lamb steaks onto a cutting board for about 5 minutes.
3. Then cut the lamb steaks into thin slices.
4. In the same skillet, add haloumi and cook for about 1-2 minutes per side or until golden.
5. In a salad bowl, add the lamb, haloumi, bell pepper, cucumber, salad leaves, vinegar, and remaining oil and toss to combine.
6. Serve immediately.

Nutrition for Total Servings:

- **Calories:** 420
- **Carbs:** 8g
- **Protein**: 35.4g
- **Fat**: 27.2g

Balsamic-Glazed Lamb Chops

Preparation time: 10 minutes
Cooking time: 15 minutes
Servings: 4
Ingredients:
Lamb chops:

- 3/4 tsp. dried rosemary
- 1/4 tsp. dried basil
- Salt and black pepper, to taste to taste
- 1/2 tsp. dried thyme
- 4 lamb chops, 3/4-inch (1.9 cm) thick
- 1 tbsp. olive oil

Balsamic reduction:

- 1/4 cup minced shallots
- 1/3 Cup aged balsamic vinegar
- 3/4 cup chicken broth
- 1 tbsp. butter

Directions:

1. Take a small-sized bowl and add the rosemary, basil, salt, black pepper, and thyme. Mix the ingredients well.
2. Place the cleaned lamb chops in a baking tray and liberally rub them with rosemary mixture. Cover the chops with aluminum foil and leave them for 15 minutes at room temperature.
3. Meanwhile, take a large-sized nonstick skillet over medium-high heat. Add olive oil to the skillet & let it heat for 1 minute.
4. Add lamb chops to the skillet and cook for 3 1/2 to 4 minutes per side until the chops are well done.
5. Once cooked, remove the chops from the skillet and keep them on a serving platter. Cover them with a plastic sheet until ready to serve.
6. Make the balsamic reduction: Add shallots to the same skillet and sauté until brown and caramelized. Add vinegar to deglaze the pan then pour in chicken broth.
7. Cook this mixture for 5 minutes on medium-high heat until the broth is reduced to half. Stir in butter and mix well.
8. Pour this balsamic reduction over the seared chops and serve warm.
9. Storage: Store in airtight container in the fridge for up to 4 days or in the freezer for up to one month.
10. Reheat in microwave, covered, until the desired temperature is reached or reheat in a frying pan or air fryer/instant pot, covered, on medium.
11. Serve: To make this a complete meal, serve the lamb chops with cauliflower mash. They also taste great paired with kale cucumber cream salad.

Nutrition for Total Servings:
- **Calories**: 256
- **Fat:** 19.4g
- **Protein:** 14.6g
- **Carbs**: 5.1g

Beef and Egg Bake

Preparation time: 5 minutes
Cooking time: 10 minutes
Servings: 1
Ingredients:

- 1 tsp. extra-virgin olive oil
- 3 ounces (85 g) ground beef, lamb or pork, cooked
- 2 eggs

Directions:

1. Begin by preheating the oven and set its temperature to 400°F (205°C).
2. Meanwhile, take a small baking pan and grease it with olive oil. Spread the cooked ground meat in the prepared pan.
3. Use a medium-sized spoon and make two holes in the beef mixture. Crack one egg into each hole.
4. Transfer the baking pan to the oven and bake it for 10 to 15 minutes.
5. Once baked, remove pan from the oven and leave it for 5 minutes at room temperature.
6. Slice and serve warm.
7. Storage: Store in airtight container in the fridge for up to 4 days or in the freezer for up to one month.
8. Reheat: Microwave, covered, until the desired temperature is reached or reheat in a frying pan or air fryer/instant pot, covered, on medium.
9. Serve: To make this complete meal, serve the egg bake with green salad or avocado. They also taste great paired with homemade keto-friendly mayonnaise.

Nutrition for Total Servings:

- **Calories:** 498
- **Fat:** 35.2g
- **Protein:** 41.1g
- **Carbs:** 2.3g

Butter Dipped Lamb Chops

Preparation time: 5 minutes
Cooking time: 10 minutes
Servings: 4
Ingredients:
Lamb chops:
- 8 lamb chops
- 1 tbsp. butter
- 1 tbsp. olive oil
- Salt and black pepper, to taste

For serving:
- 4 ounces (113 g) herb butter
- 1 lemon, in wedges

Directions:
1. Remove the lamb chops from refrigerator and leave them at room temperature for 15 minutes.
2. Use a sharp knife and make few cuts into the fat portion of the chops. Liberally, season these chops with salt and black pepper.
3. Take a large-sized frying pan and place it over medium-high heat. Add butter and olive oil to the hot pan and heat for 2 minutes.
4. Add the seasoned chops to the pan and sear them for 4 minutes per side until thoroughly cooked from inside out.
5. Transfer the lamb chops to the serving plates and garnish them with herb butter and lemon wedges. Devour!
6. Storage: Store in airtight container in the fridge for up to 4 days or in the freezer for up to one month.
7. Reheat: Microwave, covered, until the desired temperature is reached or reheat in a frying pan or air fryer/instant pot, covered, on medium.
8. Serve: To make this a complete meal, serve the lamb chops with tomato relish. They also taste great paired with crispy kale Salad.

Nutrition for Total Servings:
- **Calories:** 723
- **Fat:** 62g
- **Protein:** 43.3g
- **Carbs:** 0.3g

Steaks with Béarnaise Sauce

Preparation time: 10 minutes
Cooking time: 15 minutes
Servings: 4
Ingredients:
Béarnaise sauce:
- 4 egg yolks, at room temperature
- 2 teaspoons white wine vinegar
- 1/2 tsp. onion powder
- 2 tbsps. fresh tarragon, finely chopped
- 10 ounces (284 g) butter
- Salt and black pepper, to taste

Rib eye steaks:
- 4 (2 pounds/907 g) rib eye steaks, at room temperature
- 2 tbsps. butter
- Salt and black pepper, to taste

Salad:
- 2 ounces (57 g) arugula lettuce, chopped
- 2 ounces (57 g) lettuce, chopped
- 8 ounces (227 g) cherry tomatoes, quartered

Directions:
1. Make the béarnaise sauce: separate egg yolks from their whites and transfer the yolks to a small heat-proof bowl. Keep the egg whites for other recipes.
2. Take another small bowl and add the onion powder, tarragon, and vinegar. Mix them well and keep the mixture aside.
3. Beat the egg yolks with a hand mixer until pale in color and smooth in texture.
4. Place butter in a microwave-safe bowl and heat it for 30 seconds until completely melted. Pour the melted butter into the beaten egg yolks.
5. Rub all the rib eye steaks with butter, salt, and black pepper liberally. Then grill these steaks in the preheated charcoal grill or a pan grill until their internal temperature reaches to 145°F (63°C).
6. To serve, divide the lettuce, arugula lettuce, and cherry tomatoes into the four serving plates. Place one grilled steak on each plate and pour the warm béarnaise sauce over the steaks.
7. Serve warm and fresh.
8. Storage: Store béarnaise sauce in an airtight container in the fridge for up to 1 day and store the grilled steaks in a sealed container for 3 to 5 days in the refrigerator.
9. Reheat: To reheat, béarnaise sauce, microwave, covered, on low heat, until the desired temperature is reached and reheat the steaks in a well-greased frying pan, on medium heat.

10. Serve: To make this a complete meal, serve the steaks on a bed of baby spinach. They also taste great paired with freshly prepared cucumber dill salad.

Nutrition for Total Servings:

- **Calories:** 1124
- **Fat:** 103.1g
- **Protein**: 49g
- **Carbs:** 3.4g

Grilled Garlic Lamb Chops

Preparation time: 10 minutes
Cooking time: 6 minutes
Servings: 6
Ingredients:

- 1/2 tsp. black pepper
- 2 teaspoons salt
- 1/4 cup distilled white vinegar
- 1 onion, thinly sliced
- 1 tbsp. minced garlic
- 2 tbsps. and 1 tsp. olive oil
- 2 pounds (907 g) lamb chops

Directions:

1. Add the black pepper, salt, vinegar, onion, garlic, and 2 tbsps. Olive oil to a large-sized Ziploc
2. Bag. Shake the Ziploc bag well to mix all the ingredients inside.
3. Place lamb chops in this bag and seal it again. Shake well to coat the chops and refrigerate it for 2 hours for marinating.
4. Meanwhile, prepare an outdoor grill and preheat it at medium-high heat. And grease its grilling grates with 1 tsp. olive oil.
5. Remove the lamb chops from the Ziploc bag and discard the marinade.
6. Wrap the exposed bones at one end of the chops with aluminum foil and place them in the preheated grill. Cook the marinated lamb chops for 3 minutes per side.
7. Serve warm and fresh.

Nutrition for Total Servings:

- **Calories:** 519
- **Fat:** 44.8g
- **Protein:** 25.2g
- **Carbs:** 2.4g

CHAPTER 8:

Desserts

Slice-and-Bake Vanilla Wafers

Preparation time: 10 minutes.
Cooking time: 15 minutes.
Servings: 2
Ingredients:
- 175 grams (1¾ cups) blanched almond flour
- ½ cup granulated erythritol-based sweetener
- 1 stick (½ cup) unsalted softened butter
- 2 tablespoon coconut flour
- ¼ teaspoon salt
- ½ teaspoon vanilla extract

Directions:
1. Beat the sweetener and butter using an electric mixer in a large bowl for 2 minutes until it becomes fluffy and light. Then beat in the salt, vanilla extract, coconut flour, and almond until thoroughly mixed.
2. Evenly spread the dough between two sheets of parchment or wax paper and wrap each portion into a size with a diameter of about 1½ inches. Then wrap in paper and refrigerate for 1-2 hours.
3. Heat the oven to 325°F and using parchment paper or silicone baking mats. Slice the dough into ¼-inch slices using a sharp knife. Put the sliced dough on the baking sheets and make sure to leave a 1-inch space between wafers.
4. Place in the oven for about 5 minutes. Slightly flatten the cookies using a flat-bottomed glass. Bake for another 8–10 minutes.

Nutrition:
- **Protein:** 2.2g
- **Fat:** 9.3g
- **Carbs:** 2.5g
- **Calories:** 101

Amaretti

Preparation time: 15 minutes.
Cooking time: 22 minutes.
Servings: 2
Ingredients:

- ½ cup of granulated erythritol-based sweetener
- 165 grams (2 cups) sliced almonds
- ¼ cup of powdered of erythritol-based sweetener
- 4 large egg whites
- Pinch of salt
- ½ teaspoon almond extract

Directions:

1. Heat the oven to 300°F and use parchment paper to line two baking sheets. Grease the parchment slightly.
2. Process the powdered sweetener, granulated sweetener, and sliced almonds in a food processor until it appears like coarse crumbs.
3. Beat the egg whites plus the salt and almond extract using an electric mixer in a large bowl until they hold soft peaks. Fold in the almond mixture so that it becomes well combined.
4. Drop a spoonful of the dough onto the prepared baking sheet and allow for a space of one inch between them. Press a sliced almond into the top of each cookie.
5. Bake in the oven for 22 minutes until the sides become brown. They will appear jelly-like when they are taken out from the oven but will begin to firm as it cools down.

Nutrition:

- **Fat:** 8.8g
- **Carbs:** 4.1g
- **Protein:** 5.3g
- **Calories:** 117

Peanut Butter Cookies for Two

Preparation time: 5 minutes.
Cooking time: 12 minutes.
Servings: 1
Ingredients:
- 1(½) tablespoon creamy salted peanut butter
- 1 tablespoon unsalted softened butter
- 2 tablespoons granulated erythritol-based sweetener
- 2 tablespoons defatted peanut flour
- Pinch of salt
- 2 teaspoon sugarless chocolate chips
- 1/8 teaspoon baking powder

Directions:
1. Heat the oven to 325°F. Put a parchment paper or baking sheet with a silicone.
2. Beat in the sweetener, butter, and peanut butter using an electric mixer in a small bowl until it is thoroughly mixed.
3. Add the salt, baking powder, and peanut flour and mix until the dough clumps together. Cut the dough into two and shape each of them into a ball.
4. Position the dough ball into the coated baking sheets and flatten it into a circular shape about half an inch thick. Garnish the dough tops with a teaspoon of chocolate chips. Gently press them into the dough to make them stick.
5. Bake for 10–12 minutes until golden brown.

Nutrition:
- **Fat:** 13.2g
- **Carbs:** 5.7g
- **Protein:** 4.9g
- **Calories:** 163

Cream Cheese Cookies

Preparation time: 15 minutes.
Cooking time: 12 minutes.
Servings: 6
Ingredients:
- ¼ cup (½ stick) unsalted softened butter
- ½ cup (4 ounces) softened cream cheese
- 1 large egg, at room temperature
- ½ cup granulated erythritol-based sweetener
- 150 grams (1(½) cups) of blanched almond flour
- 1 teaspoon baking powder
- ½ teaspoon vanilla extract
- Powdered erythritol-based sweetener (for dusting)
- ¼ teaspoon salt

Directions:
1. Heat the oven to 350°F, and put a parchment paper or baking sheet with a silicone baking mat.
2. Beat the butter and cream cheese using an electric mixer in a large bowl until it appears smooth. Add the sweetener and keep beating. Beat in the vanilla extract and the egg.
3. Whisk in the salt, baking powder, and almond flour in a medium bowl. Add the flour mixture into the cream cheese and until well incorporated.
4. Drop tablespoons of the dough onto the coated baking sheet. Flatten the cookies.
5. Bake for 10–12 minutes. Dust with powdered sweetener when cool.

Nutrition:
- **Fat:** 13.7g
- **Carbs:** 3.4g
- **Protein:** 4.1g
- **Calories:** 154

Mocha Cream Pie

Preparation time: 15 minutes.
Cooking time: 5 minutes.
Servings: 10
Ingredients:

- 1 cup strongly brewed coffee, at room temperature
- 1 easy chocolate pie crust
- 1 cup heavy whipping cream
- 1(½) teaspoon grass-fed gelatin
- 1 teaspoon vanilla extract
- ¼ cup cocoa powder
- ½ cup powdered erythritol-based sweetener

Directions:

1. Grease a 9-inch glass or ceramic pie pan. Press the crust mixture evenly and firmly to the sides of the greased pan or its bottom. Refrigerate until the filling is prepared.
2. Pour the coffee into a small saucepan and add gelatin. Whisk thoroughly and then place over medium heat. Allow it to simmer, whisking from time to time to make sure the gelatin dissolves. Allow it to cool for 20 minutes.
3. Add the vanilla extract, cocoa powder, sweetener, and cream into a large bowl. Use an electric mixer to beat until it holds stiff peaks.
4. Add the gelatin mixture that has been cooled and beat until it is well incorporated. Pour over the cooled crust and place in the refrigerator for 3 hours until it becomes firm.

Nutrition:

- **Fat:** 20.2 g
- **Carbs:** 6.2g
- **Fiber:** 3.1g
- **Calories:** 218

Coconut Custard Pie

Preparation time: 10 minutes.
Cooking time: 50 minutes.
Servings: 8
Ingredients:

- 1 cup heavy whipping cream
- ¾ cup powdered erythritol-based sweetener
- ½ cup full-fat coconut milk
- 4 large eggs
- ½ stick (¼ cup) of cooled, unsalted, melted butter
- 1(¼) cups unsweetened shredded coconut
- 3 tablespoon coconut flour
- ½ teaspoon baking powder
- ½ teaspoon vanilla extract
- ¼ teaspoon salt

Directions:

1. Heat the oven to 350°F and grease a 9-inch ceramic pie pan or glass.
2. Place the melted butter, eggs, coconut milk, sweetener, and cream in a blender. Blend well.
3. Add the vanilla extract, baking powder, salt, coconut flour, and a cup of shredded coconut. Continue blending.
4. Empty the mixture into the pie pan and sprinkle with the rest of the shredded coconut. Bake for 40–50 minutes. Stop when the center moves, but the sides are set.
5. Take out of the oven and allow it to cool for 30 minutes. Place in the refrigerator and allow to stay for 2 hours before cutting it.

Nutrition:

- **Fat:** 29.5g
- **Carbs:** 6.7g
- **Protein:** 5.3g
- **Calories:** 317

Coconut Macaroons

Preparation time: 10 minutes.
Cooking time: 8 minutes.
Servings: 20–40 cookies.
Ingredients:
- 0.33 cups water
- 0.75 cups monk fruit sweetener or less to taste)
- 0.25 teaspoon sea salt
- 0.75 teaspoon sugar-free vanilla extract
- 2 eggs, large
- 3–4 cups unsweetened shredded coconut, or more as desired
- Optional: Sugar-free chocolate chips

Directions:
1. Set the oven setting to 350°F.
2. Lightly spray a cookie tin with a spritz of cooking oil spray.
3. In a small saucepan, pour in the water and the sweetener, salt, and vanilla extract. Bring to a boil using the med-high heat temperature setting. Stir and remove from the heat.
4. Use a food processor to combine the egg and coconut flakes. Pour in the syrup and process to form the dough. Using a cookie scoop, place mounds about an inch apart onto the cookie sheet.
5. Bake for 8 minutes, and rotate the baking pan in the oven.
6. Bake until lightly browned or for an additional four minutes.
7. Cool on a rack. Drizzle with melted chocolate to your liking.

Nutrition:
- **Calories:** 24kcal
- **Protein:** 0.62g
- **Fat:** 0.55g
- **Carbs:** 4.09g

Orange and Cranberries Cookies

Preparation time: 15 minutes.
Cooking time: 10 minutes.
Servings: 18
Ingredients:

- 0.75 cup butter—softened
- 3 eggs
- 0.5 cup coconut flour
- 1.5 teaspoon baking powder
- 0.75 cup monk fruit sweetener
- 0.25 teaspoon baking soda
- 0.25 cup sugar-free dried cranberries
- 0.5 cup macadamia nuts chopped
- 1.5 teaspoon dried grated orange zest

Directions:

1. In a mixing container, beat the sweetener with the eggs and butter until well combined.
2. Sift the coconut flour with the baking powder and soda. Beat on the low setting or with a spoon until fully mixed.
3. Fold in the cranberries, orange zest, and nuts.
4. Shape into rounds and arrange on the cookie sheet.
5. Arrange the cookies a minimum of one inch apart for baking on a parchment-lined cookie sheet. Press each mound down slightly to flatten.
6. Bake at 350°F until edges have started to brown or for eight to ten minutes. Cool for a few minutes,
7. Transfer to a cooling rack. Enjoy right out of the fridge for a week or they can be frozen for longer storage.

Nutrition:

- **Carbs:** 2g
- **Protein:** 3g
- **Fats:** 19g
- **Calories:** 200

Double Chocolate Chip Cookies

Preparation time: 15 minutes.
Cooking time: 8–10 minutes.
Servings: 48
Ingredients:

- 15 ounces can black soybeans
- 0.25 cup unsweetened coconut milk
- 0.25 cup cocoa powder
- 1 cup peanut flour
- 1 cup almond flour
- 1 teaspoon instant coffee granules
- 0.75 teaspoon baking soda
- 0.75 teaspoon baking powder
- 0.75 teaspoon salt
- 0.5 cup softened butter
- 0.5 cup monk fruit sweetener or erythritol
- 0.5 teaspoon stevia extract powder
- 1 egg
- 2 teaspoons vanilla extract
- 0.5 cup sugar-free chocolate chips

Directions:

1. Warm up the oven in advance to reach 375°F.
2. Drain and rinse the soybeans and puree with the coconut milk.
3. Whisk the dry ingredients, including the instant coffee, with cocoa, peanut flour, baking soda, salt, almond flour, and baking powder. Set aside.
4. Using an electric mixer, cream the butter together with the sweeteners until light and fluffy.
5. Fold in the egg and vanilla. Mix well.
6. Add the black bean puree to the butter mixture.

7. Gradually mix each of the dry ingredients into the chocolate/black bean mixture until the cookie dough just comes together.
8. Fold in the chocolate chips.
9. Drop by tablespoonful onto baking sheets, flattening slightly and adding a few extra chocolate chips on top.
10. Bake for about 8 to 10 minutes.

Nutrition:
- **Carbs:** 1g
- **Protein:** 2g
- **Fats:** 2g
- **Calories:** 34

Flourless Chocolate Cookies with Peanut Butter Chips

Preparation time: 15 minutes.
Cooking time: 8–10 minutes.
Servings: 19 cookies.
Ingredients:

- 0.75 cup monk fruit low carb sweetener powdered or 1.5 teaspoon sweet leaf stevia drops
- 0.33 cup unsweetened cocoa powder
- 1.25 teaspoon salt
- 2–3 egg whites at room temperature
- 1.5 teaspoon vanilla extract
- 0.75 cup low-carb peanut butter chips or low carb chocolate chips

Directions:

1. Warm up the oven to reach 350°F before you begin.
2. Prepare a baking sheet with a silicone mat or a layer of parchment baking paper.
3. Whisk the powdered sweetener with the cocoa powder and salt.
4. Whisk in two egg whites, one at a time, and vanilla extract.
5. Beat until it reaches a thick and fudge batter. If it's too thick, add an additional egg white.
6. Stir in chocolate or peanut butter chips.
7. Scoop the batter onto the prepared baking sheet.
8. Bake about 13 to15 minutes. Remove from the oven and cool cookies on a baking rack.

Nutrition:

- **Carbs:** 1.2g
- **Protein:** 3.5g
- **Fats:** 5g
- **Calories:** 38

Hazelnut Flour Keto Cookies

Preparation time: 15 minutes.
Cooking time: 25 minutes.
Servings: 5 servings, 20 small cookies.
Ingredients:
- 1 cup hazelnut meal ground hazelnuts
- 2 white eggs
- 1 tablespoon powdered erythritol
- 10 drops of vanilla stevia glycerite
- 1 teaspoon vanilla
- Crushed hazelnuts, to decorate

Directions:
1. Whisk the egg whites to form stiff peaks.
2. Fold in the hazelnut meal with the stevia, erythritol, and vanilla until well combined.
3. Drop by tablespoons onto a silicone baking sheet or paper-lined pan. Flatten to your liking.
4. Bake at 320°F for 25 minutes or until lightly browned.
5. Let the cookies cool and become firm before touching them.

Nutrition:
- **Carbs:** 0.4g
- **Protein:** 1.1g
- **Fats:** 3.2g
- **Calories:** 34.4

Italian Almond Macaroons

Preparation time: 10 minutes.
Cooking time: 55–60 minutes.
Servings: 45
Ingredients:

- 2 cups plus 2 tablespoons almond flour about
- 0.25 cup monk fruit low-carb sweetener
- 2 whites eggs
- 0.5 teaspoon almond extracts
- 1 tablespoon powdered (confectioner) monk fruit sweetener

Directions:

1. Combine the almond flour with the egg whites, sweetener, and almond extract.
2. Knead the mixture until the dough is formed.
3. Shape the dough into 1-inch balls and place on a parchment paper-lined baking sheet at least 1 inch apart.
4. Bake at 250°F on the bottom rack of the oven for 55 to 60 minutes.
5. Remove the cookies from the baking pan to the wire rack and dust with the confectioners' sweetener while still warm.

Nutrition:

- **Carbs:** 0g
- **Protein:** 2g
- **Fats:** 3g
- **Calories:** 31

Keto Sugar Cookies

Preparation time: 15 minutes.
Cooking time: 20–30 minutes.
Servings: 27 cookies.
Ingredients:

- 1 cup almond flour
- 0.25 cup coconut flour
- 0.33 cup monk fruit low-carb sweetener
- 0.5 teaspoon baking soda
- 0.5 cup non-hydrogenated lard or ghee/butter
- 1 egg, large
- 0.5 teaspoon vanilla extract

Optional glaze:

- 0.25 cup monk fruit powdered low carb sweetener
- Water—as needed

Directions:

1. Warm the oven to reach 350° Fahrenheit.
2. Combine each of the fixings together. Whisk or pulse together in a food processor.
3. Roll the dough out between two sheets of parchment baking paper to the desired thickness.
4. The dough can also be rolled into a log and frozen for 20 to 30 minutes. Slice into circles for easy slice-and-bake cookies.
5. Arrange on parchment lined cookie sheet.
6. Bake until the edges are lightly browned or for 8 to 10 minutes or until edges are lightly browned.
7. Remove from oven, let cool on a rack for about 5 to 10 minutes and transfer the cookies to a cooling rack until completely cooled.
8. Prepare the glaze by adding the powdered sweetener into a mixing container to make a thin glaze.
9. Divide and add the coloring as desired. Use a brush to glaze onto the cookies in a thin layer and allow to dry.

Nutrition:

- **Carbs:** 1 g
- **Protein:** 1 g
- **Fats:** 6 g
- **Cal.:** 31

Low-Carb Chocolate Chip Cookies

Preparation Time: 10 minutes
Cooking Time: 12 minutes
Servings: 36 Cookies
Ingredients:

- Softened butter (.5 cup)
- Swerve or erythritol (.5 cup)
- Stevia glycerite or stevia liquid concentrate (.25 tsp.)
- Blackstrap molasses optional (.75 tsp.)
- Egg (1 large)
- Almond flour (.5 cup)
- Low-carb vanilla whey protein powder (.5 cup)
- 12% fat - Peanut flour or coconut flour (2 tbsp.)
- Baking soda (.5 tsp.)
- Salt (.5 tsp.)
- Sugar-free chocolate chips (.5 cup)
- Optional: Chopped walnuts or pecans (.5 cup)

Directions:

1. Warm up the oven to 375° Fahrenheit.
2. Prepare the baking sheets with a layer of parchment baking paper.
3. Beat the butter in with the stevia, erythritol, and molasses until fluffy. Whisk and add the egg.
4. In another container, sift the almond flour with the vanilla whey protein powder, baking soda, salt, and peanut flour.
5. Stir all of the mixtures together until blended. Fold in the chocolate chips and nuts.
6. Use a cookie scoop to measure and drop onto the pans about two inches apart.
7. Bake until golden or about 8 to 12 minutes.
8. Cool for a couple of minutes on the cookie tin.
9. Transfer to wire racks to cool.

Nutrition:

- **Carbs:** 1 g
- **Protein:** 3 g
- **Fats:** 5 g
- **Cal.:** 74

Peanut Butter Blossoms

Preparation Time: 10 minutes
Cooking Time: 10 minutes
Servings: 24 Cookies
Ingredients:

- Sukrin Gold - packed or brown sugar replacement (.5 cup)
- Sukrin Gold Fiber Syrup or another tablespoon of Sukrin Gold (1 tbsp.)
- Natural sugar-free peanut butter or use sun butter (.5 cup)
- Egg (1 large)
- Peanut flour sesame flour for nut allergy (.5 cup)
- Baking soda (.5 tsp.)
- Vanilla extract (.5 tsp.)
- Salt (1 pinch if using unsalted peanut butter)
- Low-carb chocolate kiss drops (24) or a few chocolate chips
- Optional: Monk fruit low carb sweetener

Directions:

1. Mix the peanut butter and Sukrin Gold until well blended.
2. Prepare a baking sheet with a mat or layer of parchment baking paper.
3. Whisk and mix in the egg until incorporated. Mix in the remaining fixings until uniform dough forms.
4. Roll the dough into balls and roll in the granulated sweetener if desired.
5. Arrange on the baking tin.
6. Press each cookie ball down to about a .5-inch thickness.
7. Bake at 350° Fahrenheit until the cookies are set, about 7 to 10 minutes.
8. Allow cooling for 5 to 10 minutes.
9. Press a chocolate kiss on top of each warm cookie before serving.

Nutrition:

- **Carbs:** 1.8 g
- **Fats:** 5.3 g
- **Protein:** 3.6 g
- **Cal.:** 66

Mocha Mousse

Preparation time: 2 hours and 35 minutes
Cooking time: 0 minutes
Servings: 4
Ingredients:
- 3 tbsps. sour cream, full-fat
- 2 tbsps. butter, softened
- 1 1/2 teaspoons vanilla extract, unsweetened
- 1/3 cup erythritol
- 1/4 cup cocoa powder, unsweetened
- 3 teaspoons instant coffee powder

For the Whipped Cream:
- 2/3 cup heavy whipping cream, full-fat
- 1 1/2 tsp. erythritol
- 1/2 tsp. vanilla extract, unsweetened

Directions:
1. Add sour cream and butter then beat until smooth.
2. Now add erythritol, cocoa powder, coffee, and vanilla and blend until incorporated, set aside until required.
3. Prepare whipping cream: For this, place whipping cream in a bowl and beat until soft peaks form.
4. Beat in vanilla and erythritol until stiff peaks form, and fold until just mixed.
5. Then add remaining whipping cream mixture and fold until evenly incorporated.
6. Spoon the mousse into a freezer-proof bowl and place in the refrigerator for 2 1/2 hours until set.
7. Serve straight away.

Nutrition for Total Servings:
- **Calories**: 421.7
- **Fat:** 42 g
- **Protein:** 6 g
- **Carbs:** 6.5 g

Pumpkin Pie Pudding

Preparation time: 4 hours and 25 minutes
Cooking time: 20 minutes
Servings: 4
Ingredients:
- 2 eggs
- 1 cup heavy whipping cream, divided
- 3/4 cup erythritol sweetener
- 15 ounces pumpkin puree
- 1 tsp. pumpkin pie spice
- 1 tsp. vanilla extract, unsweetened
- 1 1/2 cup water

Directions:
1. Crack eggs in a bowl, add 1/2 cup cream, sweetener, pumpkin puree, pumpkin pie spice, and vanilla and whisk until blended.
2. Take a 6 by 3-inch baking pan, grease it well with avocado oil, then pour in egg mixture, smooth the top and cover with aluminum foil.
3. Switch on the instant pot, pour in water, insert a trivet stand and place baking pan on it.
4. Shut the instant pot with its lid in the sealed position, then press the 'manual' button, press '+/-' to the set the cooking time to 20 minutes & cook at high-pressure setting; when the pressure builds in the pot, the cooking timer will start.
5. When the instant pot buzzes, press the 'keep warm' button, release pressure naturally for 10 min, and then do quick pressure release and open the lid.
6. Take out the baking pan, uncover it, let cool for 15 minutes at room temperature, then transfer the pan into the refrigerator for 4 hours or until cooled.
7. Top pie with remaining cream, then cut it into slices and serve.

Nutrition for Total Servings:
- **Calories:** 184
- **Fat:** 16 g
- **Protein:** 3 g
- **Carbs:** 5 g

Avocado & Chocolate Pudding

Preparation time: 20 minutes
Cooking time: 10 minutes
Servings: 2
Ingredients:
- 1 ripe medium avocado
- 1 tsp. natural sweetener
- 1/4 tsp. vanilla extract
- 4 tbsp. unsweetened cocoa powder
- 1 pinch pink salt

Directions:
1. Combine the avocado, sweetener, vanilla, cocoa powder, and salt into the blender or processor.
2. Pulse until creamy smooth.
3. Measure into fancy dessert dishes and chill for at least 1/2 hour.

Nutrition for Total Servings:
- **Calories:** 281
- **Carbs:** 2 g
- **Protein:** 8 g
- **Fat:** 27 g

Cake Pudding

Preparation time: 5 min
Cooking time: 5 min
Servings: 4
Ingredients:

- ½ heavy whipping cream
- 1 tsp. lemon juice
- ½ sour cream
- 20 drops liquid stevia
- 1 tsp. vanilla extract

Directions:

1. Whip the sour cream and whipping cream together with the mixer until soft peaks form. Combine with the rest of the ingredients and whip until fluffy.
2. Portion into four dishes to chill. Place a layer of the wrap over the dish and store in the fridge.
3. When ready to eat, garnish with some berries if you like.
4. Note: If you add berries, be sure to add the carbs.

Nutrition for Total Servings:

- **Calories:** 356
- **Carbs:** 5 g
- **Protein:** 5 g
- **Fat:** 36 g

Carrot Almond Cake

Preparation time: 45 minutes
Cooking time: 15 minutes
Servings: 8
Ingredients:

- 3 eggs
- 1 ½ tsp. apple pie spice
- 1 cup almond flour
- 2/3 cup swerve
- 1 tsp. baking powder
- 1/4 cup coconut oil
- 1 cup shredded carrots
- 1/2 cup heavy whipping cream
- 1/2 cup chopped walnuts

Directions:

1. Grease cake pan. Combine all of the ingredients with the mixer until well mixed. Pour the mix into the pan and cover with a layer of foil.
2. Pour two cups of water into the Instant Pot bowl along with the steamer rack.
3. Arrange the pan on the trivet and set the pot using the cake button (40 min.).
4. Natural-release the pressure for ten minutes. Then, quick-release the rest of the built-up steam pressure.
5. Cool then start frosting or serve it plain.

Nutrition for Total Servings:

- **Calories:** 268
- **Carbs:** 4 g
- **Fat:** 25 g
- **Protein:** 6 g

Chocolate Lava Cake

Preparation time: 20 minutes
Cooking time: 10 minutes
Servings: 4
Ingredients:
- ½ cup unsweetened cocoa powder
- ¼ cup melted butter
- 4 eggs
- ¼ tsp. sugar-free chocolate sauce
- ½ tsp. sea salt
- ½ tsp. ground cinnamon
- Pure vanilla extract
- ¼ cup Stevia
- Also Needed: Ice cube tray & 4 ramekins

Directions:
1. Pour one tbsp. of the chocolate sauce into four of the tray slots and freeze.
2. Warm up the oven to 350°Fahrenheit. Lightly grease the ramekins with butter or a spritz of oil.
3. Mix salt, cinnamon, cocoa powder, & stevia until combined. Whisk in the eggs – one at a time. Stir in the melted vanilla extract and butter.
4. Fill each of the ramekins halfway & add one of the frozen chocolates. Cover the rest of the container with the cake batter.
5. Bake 13-14 min. When they're set, place on a wire rack to cool for about five minutes. Remove and put on a serving dish.
6. Enjoy by slicing its molten center.

Nutrition for Total Servings:
- **Calories:** 189
- **Carbs:** 3 g
- **Protein:** 8 g
- **Fat:** 17 g

Glazed Pound Cake

Preparation time: 1 hour
Cooking time: 1 hours
Servings: 16
Ingredients:

- ½ tsp. salt
- 2 ½ cup almond flour
- ½ cup unsalted butter
- 1 ½ cup erythritol
- 8 unchilled eggs
- ½ tsp. lemon extract
- 1 ½ tsp. vanilla extract
- 1 ½ tsp. baking powder

The Glaze:

- ¼ cup powdered erythritol
- 3 tbsp. heavy whipping cream
- ½ tsp. vanilla extract

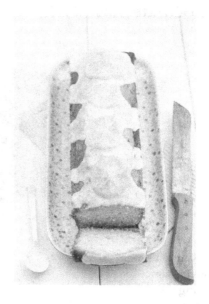

Directions:

1. Warm the oven to 350°Fahrenheit.
2. Whisk together baking powder, almond flour, and salt
3. Cream the erythritol, butter. Mix until smooth in a large mixing container.
4. Whisk and add the eggs with the lemon and vanilla extract. Blend with the rest of the ingredients using a hand mixer until smooth.
5. Dump the batter into a loaf pan. Bake for one to two hours.
6. Prepare a glaze. Mix in vanilla extract, powdered erythritol, and heavy whipping cream until smooth.
7. You should let the cake cool completely before adding the glaze.

Nutrition for Total Servings:

- **Calories:** 254
- **Carbs:** 2.5 g
- **Protein:** 7.9 g
- **Fat:** 23.4 g

Lemon Cake

Preparation time: 1.5 hours
Cooking time: 2 hours
Servings: 8
Ingredients:

- ½ cup coconut flour
- 2 tsp. baking powder.
- 1 ½ cups almond flour
- 3 tbsp. Swerve (or) Pyure A-P.
- ½ tsp. Xanthan gum
- ½ cup whipping cream
- ½ cup melted butter
- 2 lemons zested & juiced
- 2 Eggs

Ingredients for the Topping:
- 3 tbsp. Pyure all-purpose/Swerve
- 2 tbsp. lemon juice
- ½ cup boiling water
- 2 tbsp. melted butter
- Suggested: 2-4-quart slow cooker

Directions:
For the Cake:
1. Mix the dry ingredients in a container.
2. Whisk the egg with the lemon juice and zest, butter, and whipping cream.
3. Whisk all of the ingredients and scoop out the dough into the prepared slow cooker.

For the Topping:
1. Mix all of the topping ingredients in a container and empty over the batter in the cooker.
2. Place the lid on the cooker for two to three hours on the high setting.
3. Serve warm with some fresh fruit or whipped cream.

Nutrition for Total Servings:
- **Calories:** 350
- **Carbs:** 5.2 g
- **Protein:** 7.6 g
- **Fat:** 33 g

Spice Cakes

Preparation time: 15 minutes
Cooking time: 10 minutes
Servings: 12
Ingredients:
- ½ cup salted butter
- ¾ cup erythritol
- 4 eggs
- 1 tsp. vanilla extract
- ¼ tsp. ground cloves
- 2 tsp. baking powder
- ½ tsp. allspice
- ½ tsp. nutmeg
- 2 cups almond flour
- ½ tsp. cinnamon
- ½ tsp. ginger
- 5 tbsp. water
- Also Needed: Cupcake tray

Directions:
1. Warm the oven temperature to 350°Fahrenheit. Prepare the baking tray with liners (12).
2. Mix the butter and erythritol with a hand mixer. Once it's smooth, combine with two eggs and the vanilla. Add the rest of the eggs and mix well.
3. Grind the clove to a fine powder and add with the rest of the spices. Whisk into the mixture. Stir in the baking powder and almond flour. Blend in the water. When the batter is smooth, add to the prepared tin.
4. Bake for 15 minutes. Enjoy any time.

Nutrition for Total Servings:
- **Calories:** 277
- **Carbs:** 3 g
- **Protein:** 6 g
- **Fat:** 27 g

Vanilla-Sour Cream Cupcakes

Preparation time: 20 minutes
Cooking time: 25 minutes
Servings: 12
Ingredients:

- 4 tbsp. butter
- 1 ½ cups Swerve or your favorite sweetener
- ¼ tsp. salt
- 4 eggs
- ¼ cup sour cream
- 1 tsp. vanilla
- 1 cup almond flour
- 1 tsp. baking powder
- ¼ cup coconut flour

Directions:

1. Warm the oven at 350°Fahrenheit.
2. Prepare the butter and sweetener until creamy and fluffy using the mixer.
3. Blend in the vanilla and sour cream. Mix well.
4. 1 at a time, fold in the eggs.
5. Sift and blend in both types of flour, salt, and baking powder.
6. Divide the batter between the cups.
7. Bake for 20 to 25 minutes. Times may vary according to your oven hotness.
8. Cool completely and place in the fridge for fresher results.

Nutrition for Total Servings:

- **Calories:** 128
- **Carbs:** 2 g
- **Fat:** 11 g
- **Protein:** 4 g

Browned Butter Chocolate Chip Blondies

Preparation time: 20 minutes
Cooking time: 15 minutes
Servings: 16
Ingredients:

- ½ cup butter
- 2 cups almond flour
- ¼ cup Swerve sweetener
- 1 tsp. baking powder
- ½ tsp. salt
- ¼ cup Sukrin or more swerve + molasses 2 tsp.
- 1 large egg
- 1/3 cup sugar-free chocolate chips
- ½ tsp. vanilla extract
- Also needed: 9x9-inch baking pan

Directions:

1. Set the oven temperature at 325°F. Lightly grease the pan.
2. Toss the butter into the pan using the medium temperature setting. Cook until the butter is melted and becomes a deep amber (4-5 min.).
3. Remove pan from the burner to cool.
4. Whisk the almond flour with the salt, baking powder, and sweeteners.
5. Whisk the egg & add it to the mixture with the browned butter and vanilla extract until thoroughly combined. Fold in the chocolate chips.
6. Press dough evenly in the prepared pan.
7. Set a timer to bake for 15-20 minutes or until just set and golden brown.
8. Let the blondies cool in the pan. Slice into squares and serve as desired.

Nutrition for Total Servings:

- **Calories:** 161
- **Carbs:** 3 g
- **Protein:** 3.8 g
- **Fat:** 14.4 g

Key Lime Bars

Preparation time: 30 minutes
Cooking time: 20 minutes + chilling time (1 hr.)
Servings: 16
Ingredients:
The Crust:

- 1 ¼ cups almond flour
- 1/3 cup Swerve sweetener
- ¼ tsp. salt
- ¼ cup melted butter

The Filling:

- 2 tsp. lime zest
- 1 cup sugar-free oat milk
- 4 egg yolks
- 6 tbsp. key lime juice
- Also suggested: 8x8-inch baking pan

Directions:
The Crust:

1. Warm the oven to 325°F.
2. Whisk the almond flour with the salt and sweetener.
3. Melt the butter and add to the mixture to make the batter.
4. Pour the batter into the pan. Press firmly into the bottom.
5. Bake 'til just golden brown around the edges (for 12-15 min.).
6. Transfer to the countertop to cool.

The Key Lime:

1. Lime zest until creamy smooth.
2. Whisk and fold in the egg yolks until well mixed.
3. Slowly pour in the juice from the lime and oat milk. Stir until the filling is creamy smooth.
4. Add the filling into the crust. Bake it for 15-20 minutes.
5. Remove and cool. Store in the fridge for one hour to set.
6. Top with lightly sweetened whipped cream and lime slices if desired.

Nutrition for Total Servings:
- **Calories:** 188
- **Carbs:** 2.4 g
- **Protein:** 3.4 g
- **Fat:** 17.5 g

Raspberry Fudge

Preparation time: 1 hour and 15 minutes
Cooking time: 1 hour
Servings: 12
Ingredients:

- 1 cup butter
- ¼ cup white sugar substitute
- 6 tbsp. unsweetened cocoa powder
- 2 tbsp. heavy cream
- 2 tsp. vanilla extract
- 1 tsp. raspberry extract
- 1/3 cup chopped walnuts

Directions:

1. Put the butter in the mixing bowl with the mixer.
2. When smooth, mix with the rest of the ingredients until well incorporated.
3. Microwave using the high setting for 30 seconds. Blend with the mixer again until smooth.
4. Empty into the prepared pan (1-inch layer). Cover & chill for two hours in the fridge.
5. Slice into 12 portions.
6. Serve and enjoy or store in the fridge for a delicious treat later.

Nutrition for Total Servings:

- **Calories:** 242
- **Carbs:** 4.4 g
- **Protein:** 2.6 g
- **Fat:** 25.3 g

Sunflower Seed Surprise Cookies

Preparation time: 15 minutes
Cooking time: 10 minutes
Servings: 12
Ingredients:

- 1 large egg
- ¾ cup sugar-free sunflower seed butter
- 1 rounded tbsp. coconut oil
- Optional: 1 tbsp. Truvia
- ½ tsp. vanilla extract
- 1 tbsp. salt
- 1 tbsp. baking powder & soda

Directions:

1. Warm the oven temperature setting to 350°Fahrenheit. Set the rack in the upper portion of the oven.
2. Prepare a cookie tray using a layer of parchment baking paper.
3. Mix the ingredients in a large container.
4. Roll and flatten the mixture into 12 balls about the width of a quarter.
5. Bake the cookies for seven to nine minutes until they're firm in the center.
6. Cool the cookies for a couple of hours.

Nutrition for Total Servings:

- **Calories:** 69
- **Carbs:** 0.64 g
- **Protein:** 2.3 g
- **Fat:** 6.3 g

Keto Pie Crust

Preparation time: 10 minutes
Cooking time: 20-30 minutes
Servings: 10
Ingredients:

- Salt ¼ tsp.
- Butter - melted ¼ cup
- Almond flour 1
- Coconut flour 1 ½ tps

Directions:

1. Whisk the salt, sweetener, and flour in a mixing container. Fold in the melted butter to form coarse crumbs.
2. Dump it into a pie plate and press it firmly to the sides and bottom. Prick it using a toothpick or fork.

For unfilled Crust:

1. Bake 325° Fahrenheit for about 20 minutes.

For filled Crust:

1. Pre-bake it for 10-12 minutes before adding the ingredients. Cover the edges to avoid over-browning.

Nutrition for Total Servings:

- **Carbs:** 1.8 g
- **Calories:** 187
- **Fat:** 12.7 g
- **Protein:** 3.7 g

Delicious Cake

Preparation time: 30 minutes
Cooking time: 22 minutes
Servings: 12
Ingredients:

- 2 eggs
- 2 tsp. vanilla extract
- 1 ½ cups sour cream
- ½ cup Splenda granules/another keto-friendly sweetener
- 2 tbsp. melted butter
- 2 tsp. raspberry flavoring
- Also Needed: 12 ramekins or 10-inch spring form pan

Directions:

1. Warm the oven temperature at 350°Fahrenheit.
2. Whisk the eggs, vanilla, sour cream, and Splenda in a large mixing container. Work in the butter.
3. Spoon and combine about 1/2 cup of the mixture into another bowl and add the raspberry flavoring.
4. Spoon the rest of the mix into the chosen container.
5. Scoop a spoon of the raspberry batter over the top. Swirl it through the plain mixture.
6. Prepare a crust from 1/4 cup of Splenda, 1/4 cup of butter, and 1 1/2 cups ground almonds. Mix it like a graham cracker crust and add it to the ramekins/pan.
7. Arrange the ramekins in a water bath (a shallow pan with water) in the oven below the ramekins/pan.
8. Bake for 20-25 minutes for ramekins or 35-40 minutes in a spring form pan. The cake will firm up when refrigerated.
9. Top it off using raspberries and whipped cream - but add the carbs. Freeze if desired.

Note: The nutritional calculations do not include crust.

Nutrition for Total Servings:

- **Calories:** 231.8
- **Carbs:** 3.4 g
- **Protein:** 4.9 g
- **Fat:** 22.3 g

Cocoa Brownies

Preparation time: 20 min
Cooking time: 40 min
Servings: 9 servings
Ingredients:
- 1/2 cup salted butter, melted
- 1 cup granular Swerve sweetener
- 2 large eggs
- 2 tsp. vanilla extract
- 12 squares unsweetened baking chocolate, melted
- 2 tbsp. coconut flour
- 2 tbsp. cocoa powder
- 1/2 tbsp. baking powder
- 1/2 tsp. salt
- 1/2 cup walnuts, chopped (optional)

Directions:
1. Now, preheat the oven to 350°F.
2. Spray square baking pan with cooking spray or grease pan well with butter.
3. In a large mixing bowl, use an electric mixer or whisk and mix together butter and sweetener.
4. Add the eggs and vanilla extract to bowl and mix with an electric mixer for 1 minute until smooth.
5. Add melted chocolate & stir with a wooden spoon or spatula until the chocolate is incorporated into the butter mixture.
6. In separate bowl, mix the dry ingredients (remaining ingredients besides walnuts) until combined.
7. Add dry ingredients into the bowl with the wet ingredients and stir with a wooden spoon until combined.
8. Add walnuts if desired.
9. Pour batter into prepared pan. Spread to cover an entire bottom of the pan and into corners.

10. Place in a center rack of the oven & bake for 30 minutes.
11. After the brownies are baked, take them out and leave them in the pan to cool.
12. When cool, cut them into 9 servings, and they are ready to eat.

These have to be a once-in-a-while treat because they are sweet, and if you're like me, that sugar will continue to call your name. These are so good you will have to work to eat only one serving.

Nutrition for Total Servings:

- **Calories:** 201
- **Carbs:** 5g
- **Protein:** 3g
- **Fat:** 19g

Chocolate Chip Cookies

Preparation time: 10 minutes
Cooking time: 30 minutes
Servings: 24 cookies
Ingredients:

- 1 1/2 c almond flour
- 1 tsp. baking powder
- 1/2 tsp. salt
- 1/2 cup butter, softened
- 1/2 cup stevia
- 1 tsp. vanilla extract
- 1 large egg
- 1 cup sugar-free chocolate chips
- 1/2 cup nuts, chopped

Directions:

1. Now, preheat the oven to 350°F.
2. Grease cookie sheets with butter & set aside.
3. In large bowl, cream butter and stevia.
4. Add the large egg and vanilla extract to the butter and stevia.
5. Mix until the egg is incorporated into the butter.
6. In a second bowl, mix together almond flour, baking powder, and salt until mixed well.
7. Add ingredients to the large bowl & mix until it is combined.
8. Add sugar-free chocolate chips and nuts and stir until they are distributed evenly.
9. Drop by spoonful onto the cookie sheet.
10. Bake until golden brown and the surface of cookies appear dry on the top and are cooked all the way through.
11. Remove the cookies from the sheet to a wire rack to cool.

Note: Make these with or without nuts. Cocoa nibs can be used in place of sugar-free chocolate chips. This is a good recipe to keep on hand so you can have a cookie along with everyone else. Make it a fun project with kids or friends. Baking is always a good way to bring people together, and this a recipe everyone will enjoy.

Nutrition for Total Servings:

- **Calories:** 120
- **Carbs:** 3g
- **Protein:** 2g
- **Fat:** 11g

Keto Brown Butter Pralines

Preparation time: 10 minutes
Cooking time: 16 minutes
Servings: 10 servings
Ingredients:
- 2 sticks salted butter
- 2/3 cup heavy cream
- 2/3 cup monk fruit sweetener
- 1/2 tsp. xanthan gum
- 2 cup pecans, chopped
- Sea salt

Directions:
1. Line a cookie sheet with parchment paper or use a silicone baking mat.
2. In a medium-size, medium weight saucepan, brown the butter until it smells nutty. Don't burn the butter. This will take about 5 minutes.
3. Stir in heavy cream, xanthan gum, and sweetener.
4. Take the pan off the heat & stir in the nuts.
5. Place pan in the refrigerator for an hour.
6. Stir the mixture occasionally while it is getting colder.
7. After an hour, scoop the mixture onto the cookie sheets and shape into cookies.
8. Sprinkle with sea salt.
9. Refrigerate on cookies sheet until the pralines are hard.
10. After the cookies are hard, transfer them to an airtight container in the refrigerator.

Nutrition for Total Servings:
- **Calories:** 338
- **Carbs:** 1g
- **Protein:** 2g
- **Fat:** 36g

Chocolate and Nut Butter Cups

Preparation time: 35 minutes
Cooking time: 2 minutes
Servings: 6
Ingredients:
- 1-ounce chocolate, unsweetened
- 1/3 cup stevia
- 1 stick of unsalted butter
- 4 tbsps. peanut butter
- 2 tbsps. heavy cream

Directions:
1. Take a medium-sized bowl, place unsalted butter in it, and then microwave for 1–2 minutes until butter melts, stirring every 30 seconds.
2. Add stevia, peanut butter, and cream, and then stir until combined.
3. Take a muffin tray, line six cups with a cupcake liner, fill them evenly with chocolate mixture, and freeze for a minimum of 30 minutes until firm.
4. Serve straight away.

Nutrition for Total Servings:
- **Calories:** 120 Cal
- **Fat:** 17 g
- **Carbs:** 5 g
- **Protein:** 9 g

Conclusion

Now that you are familiar with the Keto diet on many levels, you should feel confident in your ability to start your own Keto journey. This diet plan isn't going to hinder you or limit you, so do your best to keep this in mind as you begin changing your lifestyle and adjusting your eating habits. Packed with good fats and plenty of protein, your body is going to go through a transformation as it works to see these things as energy. Before you know it, your body will have an automatically accessible reserve that you can utilize at any time. Whether you need a boost of energy first thing in the morning or a second wind to keep you going throughout the day, this will already be inside of you.

As you take care of yourself through the afterward few years, you can feel great knowing that the Keto diet aligns with the anti-aging lifestyle you seek. Not only does it keep you looking great and feeling younger, but it also acts as a preventative barrier from various ailments and conditions. The body tends to weaken as you age, but Keto helps keep a shield up in front of it by giving you plenty of opportunities to burn energy and create muscle mass. Instead of taking the things you need to feel great, Keto only takes what you have in abundance. This is how you will always end up feeling your best each day.

Arguably one of the best diets around, Keto keeps you feeling great because you have many meal options! There is no shortage of delicious and filling meals you can eat while you are on any Keto diet plans. You can even take this diet with you as you eat out at restaurants and friends' houses. As long as you can remember the simple guidelines, you should have no problems staying on track with Keto. Cravings become almost non-existent as your body works to change the way it digests. Instead of relying on glucose in your bloodstream, your body switches focus. It begins using fat as soon as you reach the state of ketosis that you are aiming for. The best part is, you do not have to do anything other than eating within your fat/protein/carb percentages. Your body will do the rest on its own.

Because this is a way that your body can properly function for long periods, Keto is proven to be more than a simple fad diet. Originating with a medical background for helping epilepsy patients, the Keto diet has been tried and tested for decades. Many successful studies align with the knowledge that Keto works. Whether you are trying to be on a diet for a month or a year, both are just as healthy for you. Keto is an adjustment, but it will continue benefiting you for as long as you can keep it up. Good luck on your journey ahead!

CPSIA information can be obtained
at www.ICGtesting.com
Printed in the USA
BVHW041206080621
609008BV00005B/1432